Moving Along

If The Only Choice Is To Be Strong

K.R. Sharp

Copyright © 2023 by K.R. Sharp

K.R. Sharp

Dedication

My family, whom I always miss. My
kids, who never cease to amaze me,
I am blessed to have you with me
after long years of separation.

In memory of

My beloved parents

To you who read my book. Your interest in my
work profoundly humbles me, and I want to thank
you for your dedication to the story. Your support
has been invaluable, and I cannot thank you
enough for your enthusiasm and encouragement.

Connect with the author through
email: krsreads@gmail.com or
Instagram @krsreads

Book Description

"Moving Along: If the Only Choice Is to Be Strong" is an inspirational and motivational book prepared for those with doubts about change, emotional troubles, serious crisis baggage, and no hope of moving forward in life. Are you suffering because of the loss you have experienced? This book shows how you can be resilient and hopeful. It can also help you to work towards change and be decisive to achieve freedom, happiness, and peace of mind. Each chapter contains details about what you may be going through and what you can do to deal with it. It gives information about how having resentment is normal, offers validation of anger and frustration due to the circumstances, offers reconstruction and working through to feel a sense of control over life again, and gives the motivation to shift

energy for the better. In the book are true stories about several individuals who once faced challenges but lived above them to become an inspiration to millions of people around the world. The idea is if they could do it, why cannot you?

Table of Contents

MOVING ALONG

Introduction

Have you heard of Bethany Hamilton? In the world of surfing, she remains a significant reference point. She got her left-hand bit off by a shark while surfing and lost more than sixty percent of her blood in the tragic incident when she was thirteen. However, she refused to let the storm kill her dream, belief, and passion but lived beyond it to become an inspiration to millions of Americans and the world at large. In one of her quotes, she says: "Doing everything with one arm, being well-known, and having a book and a movie, it's abnormal. As far as just not having to worry about past experiences, I've healed very well."

In Bethany's dealings in life, she opens herself up to understanding the basic principles of existence, which helps her scale through the hurdles to becoming the best version of herself. The main point is that challenges and struggles in life are inevitable. But, despite the exhaustion that comes with them, putting out all your energy to stand with your beliefs comes with a positive change.

As you step out into your daily life, it is sacrosanct that you make vital decisions on different issues (big or small) to stand firm, conquer your doubts about change, and overcome troubles. These issues are usually related to relationships, work, and personal struggles in this modern age. Yet, at the same time, if you're heavy-laden and stuck in life, you must know the appropriate solutions that can boost your optimism and resilience to drive you toward achieving your goal.

Present-day society has been given a unique definition; individualism is chiefly stressed.

Most people care only about themselves and leave others to decide their fate. Rarely will you see anyone interested in sharing the pains of others; all they care about is how they can stay conspicuous and relevant among the crowd. This shouldn't be astonishing since such feelings seem deeply rooted in human nature. We have an array of emotions, which could either fall on the strong side or in the class of weakness; these can mainly influence our dispositions toward different unfathomable circumstances. Under this, you will see how psychologists, therapists, and even counselors make themselves available to help people achieve mental and emotional stability.

I remember when I was still under the chains of the pain that life subjected me to. Our family a good example of the unfortunate; life turned out bad for us. We lost our eldest child to a vehicular accident right before she was eight. The situation got rockier after that as my ex-husband proceeded to do unacceptable acts while I was carrying our third child. After two years of struggling intensely to hold the family together, we later went through the separation process. As fate would have it, we eventually divorced. To be plain, the situation was so traumatizing. However, my emotions revealed that there was more to life than gallivanting around; it showed me that sometimes life could be difficult. But now, I am more than proud not to have given up but to stay strong and optimistic.

There is something about life itself; you can never tell where your challenge will come from. Sometimes, the person we love most may be the one who will hurt us the most. Oh! My dear, this can be saddening. But that is life for you. And the honesty is that most times, we tend to conceal it with a smile, pretending to be okay and showing an act that everything is perfect. But in our hearts, we fear change, mainly what the future may hold. Fine, there is nothing wrong with being scared. However, what you need when experiencing this silent agony is self-control to be able to do the things that are required to be done.

Martin Luther King Jr. said, "Our problem is not to be rid of fear but rather to harness and master." The worst that could happen to you is accepting to live half alive while you can be more. This is not an innovative idea; you're worth more than that. You should not let your present unpleasant situation define your future. You must make a vital decision today to effect a positive change, get over your bad experiences, stay undistracted, and empower yourself to actualize your dreams. Fear is a powerful emotion if it is used positively to your advantage. It can motivate you to act, to be more courageous, and to push beyond your abilities. It can also be a red flag which is a sign that something is wrong and that steps are needed to protect yourself. The point is to recognize when fear is valuable and when it is destructive. Learn to use fear to your advantage by understanding it, facing the situation, and learning to control it. You can also use positive reinforcement through people who are close to you or the environment to help overcome fears. By focusing on the positive aspects of a situation, you can reduce fear and anything that feels unpleasant, thus increasing confidence. Doing relaxation techniques to help manage fear and stay calm in difficult situations could alleviate the emotion. By learning to master fear, you can use it to your advantage and get better results and success in life.

This book contains every crucial point you need to achieve freedom, happiness, and peace of mind. You should prepare your mind as you learn to be resilient, hopeful, subservient to change, and strong amidst the rough waters.

Chapter One

Resentment, Is It Normal!

"I eventually understood that in harboring the anger, bitterness, and resentment towards those that had hurt me, I was giving the reins of control over to them. I was allowing them to continue to have power over me, even though they had already done their damage. I let them influence my life negatively, even though they were no longer in it. Forgiving was not about accepting their words and deeds. Forgiving was about letting go and moving on with my life. I had to take back the reins of control and take back my power. I had to take back my life and make it

my own. In doing so, I had finally set myself free".

Resentment is a toxic and destructive emotion that does nothing but breed animosity and doubt. It can damage relationships, hinder productivity, and leave one feeling helpless, hopeless, and depressed. Rather than cause resentment, it is best to take a proactive approach to address the perceived wrongdoings of others. Being patient and understanding while allowing forgiveness and resolution to be the primary objectives can help to rid resentment in the long run, allowing one to reap the rewards of happier, healthier, and more fruitful interpersonal relationships.

Tyler Perry was abused sexually and physically when he was a kid, but he rose to stardom with his unique ability to let go of the painful past. He said in one of his interviews that he could go, in his mind, to a park that his mom and aunt had taken him to, where he had a fun and memorable experience. Perry says, "So, every time somebody was doing something to me that was horrible, that was awful, I could go to this park in my mind until it was over." Tyler knows that holding onto the pain of the past could do nothing but stop him from focusing on what the future has to offer. So, he decides to channel his thought into something significant to help him eliminate his resentment toward others.

In younger years, you would have some moments that gave you joy and made you ecstatic. These were your favorite playlists saved unconsciously in your head, and you could feel good whenever you revisit these memories. It's important to remember that it's okay not to be okay. It's normal to have bad days; giving yourself the space to feel whatever emotions come up is essential. It's a must to take care of yourself. Make sure you're getting enough sleep, eating healthy, and exercising. Taking time for yourself to do something you enjoy can also help. You could up the not-so-good days through them, just like Tyler. This is because these memories contain events that strengthen your hope that one of these days, things will turn out to be different and glorious. But since hope is outrightly an expectation, you may be forced to ask, "WHEN?" At this juncture, your mind would become weary, and spiral rejection thoughts can come in, ideas that could destroy the positivity of what is set to happen.

It can also be helpful to reach out to friends and family. Moreover, talking to someone who understands can help you feel less alone and provide a different perspective and upliftment. It's also important to practice self-compassion and prioritize yourself. Remind yourself that you're doing the best you can and that it's okay to make mistakes sometimes. Focus on the present moment and practice gratitude which is imperative. Having an appreciation for the good things in your life can help you stay positive.

Life is grey. It is attributed to an uncertain, indistinct, and disputed quality. It features both highs and lows. You have no power over which one to select, as life chooses any and throws them at you. And when life happens, you need to accept things and move on.

You may want to think of this, "how precious will it be to enjoy every day passing by without having to fret?" I tell you, life would be so much simpler. The world we live in would be so much happier. Nonetheless, the most pressing query is how much of these are you letting go? Yes, I will repeat that "you are letting go." Do you still have feelings of emptiness and the lack of spark embedded inside your soul? I need to be honest with you. That's not good. It is not very good. Deep inside, you know that all these are true, yet you find it hard to dismiss. You understand that it's frustrating, yet you find it difficult to repel. This is a simple definition of resentment.

To be candid, it seems that having resentment is normal due to the daily pattern of life. However, you must understand that using resentment as a coping mechanism to deal with complex and painful emotions can be soothing for a short time but damaging in the long run. Several unhealthy things can trigger resentment. Some of these include not being heard or fear of avoidance, being taken advantage of by another, unrealistic expectations of others, feeling put down/inadequate, feelings of regret/remorse, and an inability to stop thinking about the events. These caused tense emotions/inability to let go of anger and being in relationships with a narcissist or an uneasy relationship. If you still carry resentment everywhere, you constantly feel various emotions, such as bitterness, anger, hard feelings, and disappointment. You cannot pack these qualities in the same box with exceptional achievements.

If you ask Tyler Perry, he will tell you that the ideal favor you can do for yourself is to drop these negative feelings and press forward toward better things that can make you and those around you happy. Yes, people around you need your positive energy. The best favor you can do for yourself is to let go of any negative feelings and focus on the positive things that can bring you and those around you joy. Constantly appreciate the good things in life and be grateful for what you have. Make a conscious effort to be kind to yourself and those around you. Make time to do activities that bring you joy and make you feel good. Look after your physical as well as mental health by eating healthy, exercising, and getting enough sleep. Allow yourself to ask for help, especially when needed. There is no shame in seeking support from friends, family, or professionals.

So, what exactly can keep you moving along? Tyler discovered this early and made him an inspiration to millions in the United States and different parts of the world. You must find what can help you lay off the negative emotions. Yours may not be nostalgia like Tyler, but possibly bringing more positivity and happiness into your life by concentrating on those things that are going right, seeing things from another perspective, and being kind or mindful of others (extended compassion).

Should I tell you this? Challenges suck. At every stage of your life, you will need to put in much effort, embrace endurance, and give resilience a good space. To an extent, these three golden qualities will be tested. And trust me; you don't want to fail the tests. This is because failing often has specific consequences, which can be permanent. But if the truth must be told, it is not that easy. It will come to a point where things feel overwhelming and tiring. No matter your life stage, it is vital to put in hard work, stay determined, and remain resilient. Whether you are just starting in life, in the middle of your career, or nearing retirement, you will need to put in the effort to achieve your goals. You must have the endurance to keep going even when things get tough and the resilience to bounce back from setbacks. With hard work, determination, and stability, you can make the most of every stage of life.

Where is the light? Where is the help? Can someone out there pull you out of the brink of misery? Experiencing resentment feels like drowning slowly and deeply. It makes it hard to breathe. You may be filled with the thought, "could it be just you?" You may observe that everyone around you seems to be doing fine. Their work, relationships, and personal life look positively organized; they talk and laugh as if they are not carrying any problems. But the fact remains that everyone has challenges they are battling with. That you only see the things about them looking great doesn't mean they, too, don't cry. You must avoid distractions and improve yourself mentally, socially, and physically. T.A White says, "You need to get over this. You're not the only one who has faced hardships and trials. Yours may differ from the rest of ours, but each of us has horrors in our past. Holding onto this anger will do nothing but poison you against any good that might come of your situation."

It will help if you let go of this anger and resentment; it will do you good. Focus on the positive aspects of your life and the things you can control. Reflect on what you are grateful for and what makes you happy. Look for different ways to make the most of your current situation and use it as an opportunity to grow and learn. Realize that you are not alone in this. Your loved ones do care about you and want to assist in helping you. Reach out and let them know how you are feeling. Feel free to ask for help when you need it. Know that you don't have to go through this alone. Finally, remember that you are strong and capable of overcoming any obstacle. On a brighter note, you can make a difference in your life and the lives of those around you. Don't let your past define you. Instead, use it as a source of strength and motivation to move forward.

Resentment, Your Role

Oprah Winfrey says, "There is no such thing as failure. Failure is just life trying to move us in another direction." Failure can hold you back, but it is not the end of the world. It simply signifies that you must adjust the course and try something different. Failure can be looked at as an opportunity to learn and grow. It can be a tool for a stepping stone to success. Instead of seeing failure as a negative, you should view it as a chance to explore new possibilities and find a better way. You should use failure as a tool to help you reach your goals. Failure should not be seen as a sign of weakness or lack of ability. It is a sign that you are pushing and trying new things. It is a sign that you are taking risks and challenging yourself. You should embrace failure and use it to your advantage. Failure is not a dead end. It is a chance to start over and try something new. You should use failure as a learning experience to help reach your goals and never give up and always keep trying. Remind yourself that there is no such thing as failure, only opportunities to learn and grow.

The famous writer, Stephen King, was once mercilessly battered by life. As a kid, he was tormented by a nightmare and called a troubled child and paranoid. Life was heavily against him as Stephen was raised in poverty; he grew up as an alcoholic and a drug addict. To him, alcohol and drugs were a coping mechanism for his unhappiness. Stephen's publishers rejected Stephen's works multiple times, leading him to frustration. This frustration and the abuse of substances made him think of violence toward his kids, but he was able to escape the grip of these negative emotions. Instead, Stephen used his writing as his new mechanism to cope with them. This helped him tremendously to achieve exceptional success in his chosen discipline.

Rejection can be a powerful motivator. It can be a wake-up call to take action and make changes. It can also remind you to stay focused on your goals and never give up.

Frustration can be a great motivator as well. It can signify that you're pushing yourself too hard or not taking the proper steps to reach your goals. You can remind yourself to take action back and reassess your approach. The way to stay motivated is to focus on the end goal. Remind yourself why you're doing what you're doing and why it's important to you. Furthermore, ask for help or even professional help when you need it. Finally, surround yourself with people who can support and encourage you.

GH Eifert, JP Forsyth, and M McKay (2006) practice self-compassion and forgiveness. Through self-compassion, you can understand that anger and resentment stem from a state of mind and that you can choose to let it go and move on. This involves understanding feelings, being kind to yourself, and making mistakes or being wrong without judging harshly. Similarly, forgiveness allows you to recognize that you are not perfect and that mistakes are part of life. By forgiving yourself and others, you can release resentment and open up to a more positive attitude (Eifert et al., 2006).

Finally, letting go of resentment can be facilitated by expressing feelings through art, writing, music, or any other creative outlet (Eifert et al., 2006). Through these strategies, you can learn to accept what happened in the past, let go of your resentment, and move on with your life.

Sometimes, your chief foe can be you. You might have had a series of events in the past that keeps haunting you in your present. You remain in the pool of regret and find it impossible to stop blaming yourself. This is a futile control mechanism if that is what you are driving at. It can be overwhelming and gradually birth depression, self-hatred, and self-invalidation. You may be one of those individuals involved in traumatizing events as a kid or young adult. So, you are being told by your brain that what happened was your fault or that you deserved the trauma. And until the present moment, you are still living in that strange world of self-resentment, treating yourself with contempt or feelings that you are not worthy of change, happiness, and a better life. See – this is the consequence of your past.

Moreover, if you check deep down, your mind will reveal that you are giving yourself a false definition. With this, you can become defensive. Being defensive here could result in a constant battle between the good and the bad in you, but you should understand that both parts are never real mental constructs of who you are. The guilt you feel is mostly self-imposed. Even though the negative emotions in your head are not real, you are still walking in shame, which results in you harboring resentments and nurturing isolation, anger, and low self-esteem.

Breaking yourself off the bondage of resentment and focusing on your life goal should be prioritized and essential for achieving your life goals. Resentment can be a strong emotion that can hold you back from achieving your potential and can even lead to depression and anxiety. Resentment is crucial to recognize the source of your resentment and take steps to address it. This could include talking to the person who has caused the resentment or finding ways to forgive them and move on. One incredibly crucial point here is forgiveness; this needs to be clarified. That you should forgive to deal with hate or bitterness doesn't mean that you should approve or condone the resentful behavior of such a person. Releasing through forgiveness allows for a break in the cycle of violence and hate. Forgiveness does not imply forgetting what was done or said; it only means you have decided to let go of any resentment and anger. With this, your mind will become apparent, open, and receptive to novel possibilities and ideas. Besides, your mind will focus on positive feelings and thoughts.

It is also important to focus on your life goals and to take action to achieve them. This could involve setting goals, creating a plan to reach them, and taking steps to make them happen. Taking the time to focus on your life goals and get over resentment can help you move forward and achieve the life you want. Some of the ways you can deal with the feelings of resentment include forgiving, reaching out to other family members, letting go of any bitterness or anger that you may have toward them, working through your problem, spending time with positive people, giving them a chance to redeem themselves, and learning to live without them in your life.

Leon Brown says, "Let go of resentment, for it will hold you back. Do not worry about what could have been; what is to come is what matters."

In some situations, it may not be your family that you resent or your friends or other people. In this case, you can use your family as a coping mechanism; relatable situations and inside jokes are typical scenarios. Events and celebrations make it even more memorable and tighten the bond in a relationship. And through the years, there are collected memories that linger. These memories are brought out when something reminds you of them, though most of the time, they are the silly ones – you can't help to remember the tough ones as well. Some of these memories could be about the smell of the food at Christmas or Thanksgiving, the comfort in the heart of seeing people you love gathered and celebrating, the games you played, the songs you sang, the laughter you shared, and the love you felt. They are all full of life and can help you stay focused on your dream of changing and becoming happy.

Instead of thinking about events that can keep pushing out the hatred in you, you can do well by focusing such energy on remembering those days when smiles were easily shared and always painted on your face. That stage of your life when steps were lighter, and sleep was potent enough to keep you rejuvenated; think about those moments when beautiful things happened, and there was no room for complaints and resentments. Those days when everything was excellent and beautiful, and it appeared that nothing could happen that would change the splendid atmosphere. Think about those precious times when living a contented life was all you wanted. The plan you should have for yourself is to find the route to your next dream and outline meticulously, following your wishes, how they can come to reality. Remember, you need to keep moving along!

Resentment, The Role of Your Loved Ones

Today, Oprah Winfrey is among the most famous, prosperous, and successful women. As a child, she was molested many times by her uncle, cousin, and family friend. To save herself, Winfrey had to run away from home. When she was fourteen, Winfrey gave birth to a child who died long after birth. Despite her tragic past, Winfrey stayed strong and never let it hinder her from becoming the best version of herself. In one of her quotes, she says, "Breathe, let go. And remind yourself that this very moment is the only one you know you have for sure."

Family and friends are expected to be a blessing in life. They are close by, offering substantial financial, social, and emotional support. With family and friends, you should find comfort in both times of joy and distress; they play crucial roles that make life more fun and exciting. But what will you do if all you get from them is disappointment?

Could you take a deep breath in and let it out? Remind yourself that this moment is the only one you have for sure. Let go of anything that worries you and focus on the present. Feel the air on your skin, the ground beneath your feet, and the sounds around you. Be aware of the sensations in your body and the thoughts in your mind. Acknowledge them without judgment and let them pass. Now, bring your attention to your breath. Feel the air as it enters and leaves your body. Focus on the rise and fall of your chest and the sensation of your breath in your nostrils. Allow your breath to be slow and steady. As you continue to breathe, let go of any expectations or attachments. Let go of any need to control the present moment. Instead, accept it for what it is. Allow yourself to be here, at this moment, and to be.

Robert Downey Jr. claimed that he was forced by his dad when he was a kid to smoke weed. Despite all he faced while growing up in a home that tended to shrink his goal and eventually kill it, he excelled in his profession and was referred to as one of the world's most influential men. He says, "All my arduous work paid off when I landed the Iron Man role. My comeback story proves that you can always turn your life around."

What would you do when the unexpected comes knocking on your door from those expected to keep you from life's challenges? First, there are several reasons you feel resentful toward family and friends. These may include ignoring you, blaming you for their problems, criticizing you unfairly, making unreasonable demands on you, and acting selfishly. You may be in inconvenient situations, such as unemployment and homelessness, where you are all alone, and no one is interested in helping. With this, you can create your world (being on your own or not relying on anyone). And this can lead you to abandon your family and friends, which can cause misery and self-isolation and eventually stop you from growing.

When you don't have an idea how to turn a life around, try to get help when needed and reach out, there are so many resources available, and it's essential to take advantage of them. Be able to start making positive changes in life. Start going to therapy and get involved in a 12-step program. Also, start exercising and eating healthier. Moreover, focus on relationships and ensure to spend time with positive and supportive people. It's also important to be patient and to take things one day at a time. It's a process, and it takes time.

Winfrey and Downey found themselves in situations where the feeling of resentment could be justified. But they didn't carry that burden with them. Instead, they convert the negative energy into exhibiting compassion and empathy. Negative energy can manifest in many ways, such as feeling overwhelmed, anxious, or angry. It's important to recognize these feelings and take steps to manage them. This can include taking a break, talking to a friend, or engaging in a calming activity.

It's important to remember that everyone experiences negative emotions and that it's normal to feel this way. When you recognize negative energy, you can use it to become more understanding and compassionate toward others. You can also use it to practice empathy by putting yourself in someone else's shoes and understanding how they might feel.

Craig T. Nelson says, "The superpower that I would choose would be compassion. Because that's what it takes to make it through life and understanding, a give and take, it saves an awful lot of resentment." It's the ability to understand and empathize with someone else's feelings and experiences. It is the capacity to recognize and respond to the suffering of others and the willingness to put yourself in someone else's shoes and to try to understand their perspective. Even when it's complicated, being kind and generous could go a long way. Furthermore, the ability to forgive, understand and move on is part of being human and thus relative to making it through life with wisdom.

For your family, you can do well to change your feelings about them by accepting their flaws. You cannot choose your family, but you can select your feelings about them.

Harvey Mackey says, "When you wake up every day, you have two choices. You can either be positive or negative, an optimist or a pessimist. I choose to be an optimist. It's all a matter of perspective."

Resentment, Intimate Relationships

Resentment is not a respecter of any intimate relationship. It will come knocking if you give it a chance, particularly in a long-term relationship. Several things could cause it; one of these is saying something perceived as hurtful. This is common among couples that have lived together for a long time. If your partner fails to communicate openly when hurt by you, there is a higher tendency for such a partner to feel resentful. Another common cause is unbalanced power dynamics; if you feel being steamrolled over, overpowered, or unheard in your relationship, you may begin to harbor resentment toward your partner. In addition, if you feel in your relationship that you are the one constantly doing the heavy lifting such as childcare and housework, or being the one initiating intimacy and emotional connection, or being the primary breadwinner – you may begin to feel resentment toward your partner. Other things could lead to resentment, which is why you need to understand the negative emotion when it begins to take over you. Instead of allowing it to cage you, your partner can help overcome such a situation.

The person you choose to give your heart to can positively influence your feelings. When you fall in love with someone, it shows that dopamine is rushing heavily through your system – ecstatic! The feeling will be high with so much joy that you cannot wait to get more. The heart overflows with pursuit and desire – more, more – until it pushes the boundaries trying to reach the top. Everything about the person who held your heart would be beautiful; the eyes, the laughter, the touch of their skin, and even how awesome they dress up would all be captivating and seem adorable. Blind sighted! It would be too good to be true. How lucky you would say you are; what a jackpot! Finally, you have ticked one of the essential boxes in your life. You couldn't ask for more!

More so, the moment has come for you when your thoughts rally around the possibility of you living together forever with the person you cherish most and cannot live without. The fear creeps in when you know you can do nothing to keep such a beautiful love. You would persistently try your best to hold onto your conviction, work for a more substantial establishment, and own it with all your heart. You would continuously say, "Nobody is like you, darling; you are one of a kind."

If resentments cover you like the cloud covers the sky, like grasshoppers in their number cover the mountain like grass covers a stone, and like dew covers the country. Having someone who genuinely loves you can help you offload your burden of pain and bitterness toward those who have wronged you. With love, you harbor in your heart and see the source by your side daily while going through what life has to offer – your mind is assuredly secure. You can remain strong and susceptible to change; you receive comfort in believing you are not alone in life's journey.

Steve Maraboli says, "Let today be the day you stop being haunted by the ghost of yesterday. Holding a grudge & harboring anger/resentment is poison to the soul. Get even with people, but not those who have hurt us. Forget them; get even with those who have helped us." The first step to letting go of a grudge is to recognize that it is not serving you. Holding onto a grievance can be like carrying a heavy weight. It can be exhausting and prevent you from living a whole and happy life. The next step is to forgive. Forgiveness is not about ignoring the behavior of the person who hurt you but rather about releasing the negative emotions associated with the hurt. It is about letting go of the anger and resentment and allowing yourself to move on. The third step is to practice self-compassion. Be kind to yourself and recognize that you are not perfect. It is also important to realize that everyone makes mistakes and that forgiving yourself for your mistakes is okay.

Finally, it is important to practice gratitude. Gratitude can help to shift your focus away from the negative emotions associated with the grudge and can help to bring more positive energy into your life.

The Horror of the Same Spot

There is a famous story about a man that saw some elephants tied to poles while passing through an elephant camp. What caught his attention was that the trainer only used small ropes to tie their ankles rather than powerful ones due to their big sizes.

The man was astonished and curious to know why the trainer did so and even why the gigantic animals failed to break free from the small ropes; the elephants had incredible strength for such action. So, he asked, "Mister, why are the elephants not breaking free?"

The trainer smiled and responded, "While the elephants were still babies, we used the same small size of ropes for them. But since then, we have not changed the ropes. So, the animals grew up thinking that the ropes' strength was more than theirs. But, as adults, they believe the ropes can still hold them, so they refuse to fight the condition."

The story of these elephants may apply to you as an individual that has overtime learned helplessness. Your experience in life may have conditioned you to anticipate discomfort in a specific way with no plan to make it stop or avoid it. If you stay for an exceedingly long time holding onto the condition, a time will come that you will embrace it and give up on attempting to avoid the pain, even if there is room for escape.

Jeffrey Fry says, "Resentment and bitterness build the cage that only punishes ourselves." Resentment and bitterness are emotions that can control your life if you let them. They can build a cage that only punishes you. You can become so focused on the wrongs that have been done and forget to focus on the positive things in your life. You can become so consumed with anger and hurt that you forget to forgive and move on. You can become so bitter that you forget to be kind and compassionate to yourself and others. Resentment and bitterness can be hard to overcome, but it is possible. You can start by recognizing feelings and understanding why you feel the way you do. You can then work on forgiving yourself and others and focus on the positive aspects of life. You can also practice self-care and kindness and find ways to express emotions healthily. With time and effort, you can break free from resentment and bitterness and find peace and joy.

It's easy to justify how you clung to resentment, but the consequences it prepared for you are always grievous. Naturally, you will respond when you are mistreated, wronged, or betrayed by resenting the person who put you in the position. Notwithstanding, harboring pain, anger, and displeasure more than necessary can be counterproductive. Yes, it can be more of a hindrance to you than some help. The hilarious part is that while you are holding onto resentment and being weighed down by it, the person you are channeling the negative emotion toward can still be moving around, living without knowing that you are drowning in the river of unhealthy feelings. So, why do you need to cage yourself unnecessarily?

Carrie Fisher says, "Resentment is like drinking poison and waiting for the other person to die." Resentment is an emotion that can cause tremendous damage, both to the person feeling it and to those around them.

A study by GV Bodenhausen et al. (1994) examined the factors that can cause resentment and the subsequent damage it can cause. It found that a sense of injustice is crucial in developing resentment, as people feel a sense of unfairness, moral outrage, and frustration. These emotions can lead to various negative behaviors, such as revenge, aggression, betrayal, and manipulation. Furthermore, the study found that resentment can lead to a breakdown in trust and communication, devastatingly affecting relationships and community cohesion. These issues can then be compounded further if resentment is allowed to fester, leading to long-term psychological damage and an inability to form meaningful relationships. Importance to understand the causes of resentment and the damage it can cause if left unchecked. Addressing resentment can help to reduce the negative impact it can have on individuals, relationships, and the wider society.

Research from KW Springer, J Sheridan, D Kuo, and M Carnes (2007) has shown that the long-term effects of resentment on mental and physical health can be profound. Resentment can manifest in a variety of ways, including feelings of anger, bitterness, and frustration. These feelings can lead to physical and psychological problems that can last for years and significantly impact one's overall well-being. For example, resentment can lead to increased levels of stress and anxiety, which in turn can lead to an increased risk of depression, substance abuse, and other mental health problems. In addition, resentment can lead to physical health problems, including high blood pressure, heart disease, and other chronic illnesses.

Furthermore, resentment can impact relationships, leading to social isolation and difficulties with communication. These problems can further exacerbate the harmful effects of resentment on mental and physical health. Addressing these issues as soon as possible reduces the risks of this form of emotional distress.

The point is that resentment will make you stuck in the present juncture. If you stay in this spot without a personal decision to move on, it will automatically open the door to a feeling of defeat. At this stage, the statements rolling over endlessly from your mouth would be, "What's left to fight for? Nothing would make any difference." The rush of unsupportive conception usually is a norm that is hard to break as a habit. Can you still recognize the person you look at every day in front of the mirror? What has changed? I guess your answer will be nothing. This is because you have not opened yourself to the proper lifestyle that can bring about change. Breathe; you need yourself amongst anyone.

There may be an avalanche of questions about your situation that you don't yet have answers to. By defining your silence and dark thoughts, you still find it challenging to navigate that a day will come when you are angry in a life that you think is supposed to be good. Such is life; you must know. But you may still want to find answers to how it has led to what is happening in your life.

Yesterday, everything was fun; but now, what has gone wrong? Just like a snap of a finger, everything has turned against you. Oh! Life is not fair. The more you nurture these thoughts in your mind, the more anger will continue to build inside you, which can overwhelm you. You should understand that life will always, at a particular time, throw ugly things at you and make you appear lifeless, as if you are in it alone. So, you must allow all these things that come your way to help you move to where you need to be.

When life happened to me, I had every reason to give up. The pain was so intense that I thought my life was over. The guilt of losing my wonderful eight-year-old daughter in a vehicular accident was all over me; I hated myself. Even my ex-husband made the matter worse while I was carrying another child. So, yes, life has never been fair. But we are all given a decision to make, which is choosing to stay on the spot filled with bitterness, pain, anger, unworthiness, and disgust – or choosing to pick up your broken self, being optimistic and resilient, focusing on becoming a better person and living a happy life that attracts positivity.

It is high time you broke from the bondage that resentment has put you in. You cannot wait for the situation to improve; you must take action. And most chapters of this book contain them. Yes, it would help if you built a solid mindset to make things happen. You do not want to be like those elephants with the weapon to set themselves free effortlessly, but their perspective failed them by making them think they needed to be stronger. Norman

Vincent Peale says, "Never allow sick attitudes to poison your thinking, nor let ill will make you ill. Avoid making your mind sore by that painful hurt called resentment."

If you continue to give room for the fear to change, then stagnation birthed by resentment will be forced to have its way. That anger you hold onto will only paralyze you from taking any positive action.

When pain and anger from significant loss overwhelmed me, the feeling I got was one that the light in me and I were in a great battle. I knew I was turning into someone different and that the love in my heart was about to leave; I felt tired of life. But I decided to give change a chance. I accepted my new reality and proceeded toward a better course.

Learning how to cope with anger, fear, and other negative emotions such as loneliness, sadness, rejection, and self-rejection would be best. Instead of focusing on these feelings, you can embrace joy, happiness, excitement, curiosity, love, gratitude, contentment, and interest

Chapter Two

Self-Validation: Anger and Frustration

"Rather than falling into the trap of wanting an explanation or validation from the gaslighter, turn to self-validation. When you reaffirm the reality of the abuse you have experienced, you will get one step closer to healing from the narcissist. Anchor yourself in what happened, and do not let anyone rewrite reality for you." Attaching to what happened is an integral part of self-care and self-preservation. Remember that no one else can rewrite reality. It is up to you to take ownership of experiences and to remember that truth is valid. When anchoring in what happened, take a step back and look at experiences objectively. Recognize your and others' feelings and experiences without letting them define you. This allows for more openness to understanding and accepting different perspectives and more mindfulness of thoughts and feelings if they are valid and when they are not. External factors influence thoughts and feelings, and it helps to be more aware of biases and more open to different perspectives. Furthermore, being aware of triggers and more mindful of how to react to them are equally important. Boundaries for interacting with others are essential and have to be respected.

The story of Robin Klammer is a very inspirational one. She writes on Medium and happens to be a member of the Wounded Birds Ministry group on Facebook. In one of her discourses, Klammer revealed what her life was like in the past and what it is now. While talking about the meaning of validating experience, she told Wounded Birds Ministry, "Validation is a conundrum to me. I didn't feel I had much worth for so long unless someone told me I did. From my earliest years, I remember thinking, 'I'm not good unless someone else says so.' I'm not quite sure exactly when this perception came about." She narrated how she had no option but to stay in a place that could not be called home and lived with strangers with whom she could not put her trust. But to cut the story short, Klammer said, "I am profoundly grateful that I have been able to reach out and get the help I needed. That's not to say that I don't have dark moments or days/weeks, but I have better tools to deal with them. I know from whence it came. I can now validate what I'm feeling and take steps in self-care to remedy this malady."

Have you checked yourself out and discovered that you are a people-pleaser and, most times, depending on outside of yourself for validation? And while in such a situation, have you ever felt the helplessness when you tried to express your anger and frustration but ended up feeling dismissed? It would be best if you understood that your feelings and past experiences could not define who you are. When you are filled with rage, the fact is that it is not always about anger. It is mostly about how frustrated you feel or how overwhelmed and confused you are. Another thing is if you persistently embrace your uncomfortable emotions and give large room for them, you will, over time, not only feel one emotion but several of them. With this, you need to learn how to identify and label each of them correctly to gain the strength to see your experiences in a new light.

Self-validation is both valuable and acceptable. It is a skill that involves recognizing and transcending the sense of self through different means to regard the meaning and absolute value of your existence. It is a vital process if you're going through some emotional challenges that help restore and reinforce your life's intention, sense of self-worth, competence, and personal identity.

As much as you are still on this planet, self-validation should be taken as a vital process of your life. Why? Your existence comes with the job description of recognizing the value of your unique individuality. You must seek after actualizing your potential to attain the highest form of perfection in your natural environment, regardless of what people say about you. You might have heard of Shakira, the famous Columbian singer. When she was a girl, her teacher told her she could not be a singer because her voice was like a goat's. Yes, she was angry and frustrated. But she carried the vision to be the voice of all whose voices are not heard; she believed in what mattered. And do you know what? Today, Shakira's success story is a motivation to millions.

Your quest is expected to be toward restoring, maintaining, and enhancing the value of your self-worth and the meaning of your existence. In one way or the other, you have consciously and unconsciously been experimenting and exploring how to offer yourself correct validation since you were born. This is because you know within yourself that self-validation comes with several benefits. From it, you have access to security, identity, the joy of living, comfort, connectedness, self-acceptance, and more.

Nonetheless, the moment you lose the sense of your self-worth and the meaning of your life, you will open a wide door for anger, emptiness, sadness, anxiety, loneliness, pain, despair, and frustration.

But while you are overwhelmed by these feelings, you may begin to restore this lost worth and meaning consciously and unconsciously. Some cases are different; you may need to seek validation elsewhere if you experience a permanent loss of a significant source of self-validation. These may include the loss of a job or a partner. You are not ignorant that leaving self-validating conditions to interfere with your self-esteem and inner peace should not be condoned; this is because allowing them can have grave consequences on your health. To survive your situation and get enlightened, you must validate yourself correctly.

Validation Vs. Invalidation

As it has already been rightly stated in the previous paragraphs, your self-worth, identity, and the meaning of your existence are crucial parts of your life. And it is a fact that you cannot help but, at a certain point, experience some rough situations and moments that will shake these three values mentioned above. One of the everyday self-invalidating experiences you can face is being ignored or criticized. This is because your existence is basically about self-concept and social relationships. You can ask Walt Disney about this – he got fired from his first job after his newspaper editor told him that his imagination and creativity were insufficient. This seemed to be true after some years when he was responsible for driving Disney's animation studio, Laugh-O-Gram, into bankruptcy. But do you know what? His determination was intact. He pressed forward to overcome every criticism and lack of self-worth to become successful. Being criticized or misunderstood by others can be a lonely and alienating experience. It can be hurtful when others see you as unworthy and inferior to get their attention or respect. Joel Osteen says, "You must accept that some people will never be for you. Treat them respectfully, but you do not need their approval to fulfill your destiny."

When you find yourself in an environment where people never agree with your values and worldview and persistently attack you, this can bring out of you the feeling of not being validated and appreciated. As you move through life, your intimacy needs will change from requiring good protection and approval from other people to being understood and emotionally connected. When those close to you cannot offer this need, you will automatically feel the absence of spiritual self-validation. This can grow into you making mountains out of the molehill of minor incidents, sometimes via self-critical reasoning and selective perception. For instance, you may begin to see minor conditions as crisis situations, leading you to lose your competence and the value of your self-worth.

Yes, your frustration and anger from your experiences are incredible. They will be there for a long time, stopping you from focusing on how you can develop your life. These two negative emotions are the children of the loss of self-worth, competence, and the meaning of life. Several psychological processes are deemed to occur when you give room for these situations; these may include feeling you have been denied the right to feel or be during the moments. This is a time when all you feel is as if you are drowning in pain and frustration. With this, you will begin to be overwhelmed by doubt in your self-worth and lose your self-respect and confidence. You will have your self-identity shaken, becoming uncertain of who and what you are. Besides, the sight of the meaning of your life will be lost, leading to a loss of direction and hopelessness. So, tell me, how can you actualize your dream this way?

You should know that they are sometimes seen as threatening and unbearable when you battle with all these. And with this, you may employ some defense mechanisms to deal with the pain that comes with them and use self-awareness to keep yourself safe from the despair that is set to come in. Nevertheless, you must deal with the self-invalidation lifestyle or situation and seek self-validating activities and relationships. The moment you learn how you can self-validate your emotions when you feel angry, sad, or frustrated about the events that have happened around you, there is a possibility that you are coping incredibly with the overwhelming emotional process.

Furthermore, you can quickly identify invalidation when you begin to make expressions such as "I am fine," "I think I am too sensitive sometimes about issues," "I do not care about this," or "It is important that I get over this situation," "I do not have a reason to feel sad, angry, and frustrated right now," "I should not feel frustrated and upset," "I am just overreacting," or "I am such an idiot for being frustrated or angry." On the other hand, you can quickly identify self-validation when you make expressions such as "Today is a hard day for me," "The project I did today was a great job," or "There is nothing wrong with me to have said no to that person," "I do not feel like myself," "I am frustrated and sad," "I need to cry," "I am filled with joy, and that brings a smile to my face," "I understand the reason I am scared about my present situation," or "I do not feel heard by my friend."

Self-Validation, Processes

You have sat down and done a good assessment of your life. You know where you are coming from and where you are, but where you are heading is still being determined. There are several questions you must be ready to provide answers to if you intend to leave your emotionally challenging situation. These include how you can overcome the latest unpleasant experience of loneliness and self-doubt. Who is ready to give you emotional validation or support of you being a unique and valuable person? What helpful activities can you engage yourself in to regain a positive perspective on life and self-confidence? What steps can you take to divert your attention from inner pain, anger, and frustration? And what sort of self-care, lifestyle, and physical comfort can you provide yourself with? Good answers to these questions will help improve your situation and launch you toward living a happy and fulfilled life.

There are numerous available things you can opt for when facing criticism. On several occasions, I have taken some of these steps to help myself since they could effectively change my negative emotional state and give me a better one. Whenever I am criticized, I may decide to visit my intimate friend that can give me a good definition of who I am, go jogging or swim to shake the negative feelings off, think about what I have accomplished so far in my life to remind myself of how competent I am, or take a long walk, appreciating the things of nature. I can put the situation in order by doing any of these when faced with bad feelings.

It is important to also seek validation from within. This means that you accept yourself and your own decisions without relying on the approval of others. Instead, trust your judgment and be confident in your abilities. This will help to develop a strong sense of self-worth and self-esteem. Moreover, if you aim to restore and enhance the meaning of your life and how you feel about your self-worth to get rid of persistent anger and frustration, the three areas or activities of self-validation you need to investigate are personal, social, and physical. I will be delving deep into each of these later in this book.

One of the benefits of embracing validation of anger and frustration due to your circumstances is that it would not only help restore the damage negative emotions have done to your self-esteem and the meaning of your life while you were wallowing in your challenges, but also continue to be of help throughout your lifetime. That sounds good to you! Self-validation is expected to be a process that should be maintained and enhanced constantly as part of your day-to-day living. You must retain this healthy lifestyle to feel happy consistently, instill life's meaning, and learn to manage your anger, stress, frustration, and self-invalidating situations. With this, you should focus on seeking and maintaining suitable personal activities and talents, nurturing relationships, creating a pleasant and familiar environment, and incorporating exercise and a healthy diet.

In addition, you may want to keep some specific levels of validation in mind when battling negative emotions. These levels are found under Dialectical Behavioral Therapy (DBT). The first on the list is that you need to pay proper attention to the situation. If you are emotionally challenged with frustration and anger, the first thing you need to take seriously is those emotions when you are faced with the situation. Where the real work lies is practicing mindfulness; rather than pushing away your experience, this quality will help you pay attention to it. One of the common things that people do to push away, avoid, or hide their crisis is engaging in substance use. The worst part is that abusing substances will only worsen the matter. For frustration, hiding your feelings is not an advisable way to deal with it because it has physical and emotional effects. One thing that is known for sure is that these intense feelings will never go away on their own. So, you must recognize your anger and frustration and take active steps to deal with them.

Another thing you need to bear in mind is reflecting on what you do. When you reflect, the primary thing you do is give deep thought about your motives, actions, and thoughts. Your assignment here is beyond paying attention to what you feel or think; you must also describe the situation effectively. Has avoidance been your primary device to manage negative feelings? If this is the case, this step can be difficult at first. Nonetheless, if you can proceed with it, you will learn more about why you are feeling a specific emotion or even why such an emotion is making you behave the way you do. One of the questions you may ask yourself is, "What prompted me to feel sad, angry, and frustrated right now?"

Despite how vital reflection and describing your crisis is, there are times when you may find it difficult to label your feelings and thoughts accurately. This is where you will need to employ accurate guessing. Yes, it would help if you had some guesswork. Through this, you need to determine what is happening at the moment. One of the frequent questions that can come to your mind is, "When was the last time I felt this way, and what was it like?" You can introduce the first step here in this level by paying proper attention to your body language when you are sad, angry, or frustrated; this will significantly help you make an accurate guess of your feeling. When you take time to review the apparent facts, you can quickly determine the proper response you might need for such a crisis, which may be the sadness, frustration, and anger you feel after losing a job or something else.

Opting for some guesswork may be ineffective because the system may feel wrong. In this case, you should explore the understanding step. This step can help you validate your feelings and thoughts concerning the pattern from your history. Here, you can express something like, "I know I felt angry and sad when my partner left due to how I struggled with being alone."

If you must know, your emotional experience is like everyone else's. Generally, our nature as humans leaves us with the weakness to be susceptible to experiencing several emotions, which include sadness, anger, frustration, shame, anxiety, and even happiness. So, you should understand that you should avoid discrediting how you feel due to its discomfort. How can you acknowledge that your feeling is valid and authentic? You can do this by thinking about specific situations that can trigger the emotion. For instance, you can say, "I feel anxious because I have no idea what online school will be like."

Finally, one of the most important steps is being truthful. You should not deny your feelings. If an emotion comes up, try to feel it. Hiding it or lying to yourself about it will do no good but aggravate your suffering in the long run. For example, are you faced with judgmental thoughts? I will advise you not to run away from them but ask yourself, "Is giving any attention to this thought giving me the needed help to live the life I want?"

Personal Self-Validation

Do you find yourself in crisis, and all you need to lift your spirit out of anger and frustration to focus on the future ahead is to validate your self-worth and the meaning of your existence? There are several personal activities you can employ to do this effectively. These include picking an enjoyable book to read, engaging in personal projects, learning, practicing effective meditation, exploring your hobbies, taking religion seriously, listening to your favorite spirit-lifting music, focusing on sports and art, and many others. These activities can intrinsically motivate you, mainly when you are self-critical, frustrated, and upset, by providing confidence, comfort, happiness, hope, freedom, and peace of mind. Apart from the fact that these personal activities will be fun for you, they are also personally rewarding. Through them, you will learn how to control your emotions, develop your life, live a healthy lifestyle, and many more. Yes, they are personal, making you independent of craving social approval and praise — these activities feature an element of personal meaning and life.

When you are angry and frustrated, what you need most is how to be in control of and at peace with yourself; personal self-validation can offer you this. It is a process that offers the joy of competence and self-improvement and the comfort or satisfaction of being in a healthy environment that supports you in being in control and at peace with your individuality. When you engage in these personal activities, you are qualified to bask in the pleasure of feeling in a beautiful way and access a timeless flow experience. This implies that they will help you validate your spiritual and timeless self. Suppose you have ever taken part in any of these personal activities, such as reading exciting novels, meditation, star watching, nature-watching, music, and artistic and creative activities (painting, pottery, dancing, and weaving). In that case, you will understand why they are perfect for you, particularly in crises.

In addition, the intrinsic reward of engaging yourself in something personally productive and meaningful is entrenched in personally validating activities. You can access distinct moments to know and validate your spiritual, timeless, and competent self with them. Getting comfort and enlightenment may depend on the personal activities you prefer; your interest may lie in reading scriptures or novels, praying, or chanting mantras. Notwithstanding, some specific actions are significant and effective in dealing with several experiences of ego-transcendence. These include house-cleaning, singing, gardening, cooking, jogging, dancing, painting, and more.

Personal self-validation is recognizing and accepting worth and value as a person. It is the practice of validating feelings, thoughts, and actions rather than relying on external sources of validation. Moreover, it is not about seeking approval from others but rather about recognizing and accepting worth and value. Self-validation is integral to self-care and self-love and can help build a strong sense of self-esteem and confidence. Regardless of what other people may think or say. It is about understanding that they are worthy of love and respect and that feelings, thoughts, and actions are valid and vital. It is about recognizing that you can make decisions for yourself and have the right to make mistakes and learn from them. It can help build a strong sense of self-esteem and confidence and help one feel more secure in relationships. When practicing self-validation, make decisions that align with values and beliefs. Self-validation is also crucial in emotional regulation and responding healthily and constructively. This can help you manage your emotions more effectively and to develop healthier relationships with yourself and others. Self-validation is a process that takes time and practice.

Social Self-Validation

As you need others for emotional help for

mental wellness, others equally need you for the same purpose. Yes, most people surrounding you, including your partner, parents, friends, children, etc., need you, and you also need them for emotional and social survival.

Can you remember the last time you felt lost and down? The first thing that could have come to your mind is finding specific persons that could welcome you to their space and offer you emotional support for your crisis. The interesting part is that your perfection is not required with them – their significance is to accept you the way you make them unique. When you table your challenges, they will be keenly interested and willing to render care and support. Moreover, they will do this with respect. These remarkable individuals are available to listen to your hardship and joy, making you feel validated and safe.

Social self-validation is the process of seeking approval from others in order to feel good about oneself. It is a way of seeking external validation from others to feel accepted and valued. This type of validation can come from family, friends, peers, or even strangers. It can be as simple as a compliment or as complex as a full-on conversation. Social self-validation is an essential part of human development. It helps us to build relationships, gain confidence, and feel accepted. It can also help learn how to interact with others, handle difficult situations, and develop a sense of self-worth and self-esteem. However, it is essential to remember that social self-validation should not be the only source of validation.

A typical instance is when you find yourself in a strange situation and are introduced to an unfamiliar culture; this will make you know the value of communicating with someone that shares your native language. The fact is that your self-evaluation and identity are connected to cultural conditioning. So, when you have mutual intelligibility with someone because such a person shares the same value system and cultural norms with you, you will enjoy the validating experience even after battling a foreign culture as a stranger.

Moving from one particular country or city to another is a bold step. But the truth is that such a decision usually comes with a challenging experience that can lead to frustration. You can imagine how it can make you feel when you are disconnected from a well-developed and familial social support network and moved into a pristine environment. Usually, you will feel the loss of a validating and familiar relationship. Also, your vulnerability in such a unique setting will expose you to several criticisms and self-doubt, which could make you think of connecting yourself with another where you can get validated and develop a sense of self-control. This explains why losing your status or changing your present location can be devastating and frustrating.

Most times, there is a mutuality in self-validating relationships. As others need you to validate their identity and self-worth, so do you. As far as self-validation is concerned, your aim will be toward getting valued and wanted by your parents, children, colleagues, local community, customers, and so on. The secret is that when you have access to genuine care and love in a non-manipulative or non-possessive way, the possibility of experiencing a deep spiritual bond with people who are interested in making your life meaningful can be actualized. The bottom line is that even if you are drowning in your challenges, having those who love you around will help you remain optimistic about life, live a life full of meaning, and keep a balanced perspective on life situations. This is made possible when they validate your actual individuality.

Physical Self-Validation

I can touch every area under self-validation, but the elaboration will only be complete if I discuss physical self-validation. It is impossible to separate the body from the mind because both are interconnected intricately. It will not be possible for you to regain your self-consciousness if you do not regard the body and give it what it needs. How can you validate yourself physically, and what are the benefits of doing these? You can validate yourself physically by restoring adequate energy, pleasure, comfort, and familiar physical sensations.

Several activities feature attention-diverting and relaxing effects in which you can engage your body. These activities can offer mental and physical sensations related to relaxation, memories, and self-validating imageries and feelings. For example, you may be someone who, when on your own or frustrated, may tend to take a nap. This activity has been studied to have the ability to help you regain your energy, strength, and better perspective on life.

Some specific types of meals can bring into your memory your past events and your home.

For instance, if you find yourself in a foreign country as a student. Suppose you sing songs in your mother tongue, play a piece of familiar music, or cook a native meal. In that case, you can recreate a self-validating and friendly environment, particularly when you are overwhelmed with frustration, self-doubt, and homesickness.

Experts have shown how sleeping and resting are crucial. You can be guaranteed excellent wellness by observing them appropriately, along with regular dietary and physical activities. Maintaining a healthy physical condition and avoiding abuse or damage to the body requires discipline and sensitivity of care to the body. When you give room for proper physical self-discipline and the correct attitude, you are ready to welcome transcendence from an ordinary physical activity to an ego-transcending and spiritually enlightening experience. Oh! This is a beautiful place you will be positioned, as both your body and mind, will unite, and you will have access to a colorful and timeless world where you make a union with your greater self.

What are the helpful exercises you can do? Some of the great ones I recommend include body movements, solitary arts of meditation, martial arts, and dance. These do not just exercise through which you have access to incredible energy and proper physical comfort; they come with some other significant benefits to your physical and mental status. A good example is martial art; this is one of the ways you can gain mental relaxation, muscle toning, or feel better than an average person. In addition, you can take the exercise beyond the ordinary level of technical and physical training by managing the art seriously with an exceptional, timeless commitment and great concentration for integrating physical art, lifestyle, and philosophy via years of discipline and challenging work.

Nevertheless, using these arts as an easy means of escaping from experiencing some crises may put you at risk of compulsively attaching or being addicted to them. This is related to how the arts are body-oriented activities that you will find easy to focus on and derive rewarding sensations. After living in frustration and anger for so long without regard for much self-discipline, there is a tendency for you to do the extreme and turn abusive to your body.

In addition, if you overuse physical activities to escape from your painful feelings of self-doubt and self-criticism and avoid or postpone confrontation using emotional dynamics, you may develop a self-defeating lifestyle, such as drug abuse, eating disorders, and alcoholism.

Physical self-validation is the practice of recognizing and validating one's physical self.

It is a way of honoring and respecting the body and its capabilities, appreciating its strengths and weaknesses, and understanding that physical health is integral to overall well-being. Accepting the body for what it is, rather than trying to change it to fit a particular ideal, thus understanding that physical health is not just about appearance but also about how the body functions and feels.

Chapter Three

Reconstruction and Working Through Phase

Could you ever imagine that one of the most influential and powerful people in the world today was once greatly challenged by the horror of life? I am talking about Joe Biden, the President of the United States. You may know a lot about him, but this information you may have will be incomplete if you are not aware of how he suffered from grief. Yes, life came after him terribly, but he was able to fight the emotional battle victoriously to become who he is today.

The septuagenarian shows through his life experiences of loss that pain can make you find purpose. In 1972, Biden received the most tragic news; he was just thirty at that time and had just won his first senate race. The announcement came to him through a call that his partner Neilia and his one-year-old child, Naomi, had died in a car accident while going Christmas tree shopping. The other two children (Hunter and Beau) were able to survive the crash but were seriously injured.

Life never stopped happening to Biden because, after many years of losing two of the most cherished individuals in his life, Beau later lost his life to brain cancer in May 2015 at the age of forty-six. With this unfortunate event, Biden decided in 2016 not to run for president since his family was grieving. Nevertheless, he later thought moving forward with dedication would be a distinct way to honor those he had lost.

While Biden was on his campaign trail, he told people that the best thing they could do would be to find a consistent purpose, something that they may have lost but want to be doing. He elaborated that heartbreak would not fade away, but over time, he discovered how to use what had happened to him to guide those going through a similar situation.

Generally, grief is seen as a natural response to loss. Are you suffering emotionally due to losing someone precious to you? Yes, this is the perfect description of grief. Most times, the pain accompanying this loss can be so overwhelming that life may become uninteresting to you. You would feel like nothing is left for you here in this world to do;

you might even wish it had been you who was the victim of the situation. When submerged in grief, several unexpected and complex emotions will set in. These may include anger, shock, guilt, disbelief, sadness, depression, and pain.

Since grief comes with pain, your physical well-being may be disrupted, making it difficult to eat, sleep, or think properly. It feels like you have lost the most critical part of yourself or you have been cut in two; these are evident reactions when faced with loss. But you should know that the level of your loss significance determines your grief's intensity.

One of the biggest challenges you can face is trying to cope with losing something or someone you love passionately. Grieving is mainly associated with the death of a loved one. Yes, losing someone is usually the cause of the most intense type of grief. But grief can be caused by any loss, including loss of safety after a trauma, loss of a friendship, loss of a cherished dream, retirement, a loved one's serious illness, death of a pet, loss of financial stability, divorce or relationship breakup, a miscarriage, losing a job, loss of health, and selling the family home. Some subtle losses you may experience in life can make grief set in. For example, are you moving away from home, changing your job, or graduating from college? These related losses might trigger a sense of grief in you.

Now you know that grief is far beyond losing someone to death. It is considered the natural and normal emotional reaction to the change in your regular patterns of behavior. When you react to other types of loss aside from the death of someone, it is usually referred to as disenfranchised grief. Even if numerous individuals may not count the different types of grieving experiences, it doesn't erase the fact that they can influence your emotion by causing you pain.

Grief can be an overwhelming reaction that usually occurs to people without knowledge, making it extremely shocking, unbelievable, and depressing.

What we all are used to is getting knowledge of how to get things; we learn how to go and maintain a relationship, how to get a job, how to chase a dream, how to get and take care of a pet, how to accumulate wealth, how to live healthily, and so on. However, no one has taken it as a responsibility to open our eyes to what we need to do when we lose any of these wonderful things. Have you ever thought about that? And when we, fortunately, have the opportunity to have access to information about how to cope with losing these things, most of the details appear to be misinformation. They can only be of little to no assistance in our emotional crisis. Is that okay? Yes, it is. This is because both are equally important. You live in a world of uncertainty where anything can happen at any time. So, the focus should be on more than just acquiring things but also dealing with the feelings when you lose them.

There is another thing you need to know about grief – it is not intellectual but emotional. What does this mean? You see, a friend often comes to you, providing you with logical reasons to avoid feeling sad. Well, their move is right, and they are trying to help by attempting to change your perspective about your situation. But the fact is that, as a griever, what you have is a broken heart and not a broken head. So, the logical reasons they may provide you with to make you not feel sad are often unhelpful and fail to improve your feelings.

People usually believe that grief has stages. This may be right, but not true; there are no stages. You can feel numb when you get news about losing someone you love. During grief, you may feel disconnected from others and be emotionally blank. You may experience this if you find it difficult to process your emotions properly or feel guilty because you cannot show an emotional response or cry about your loss. You should remember that if your relationship with the person or the thing you have lost were extremely unique, the way you will grieve would equally be unique. When you feel numb as a part of the grieving process, I will advise you to stop or avoid judging yourself and allow the emotions to come how and when they will.

Furthermore, you tend to suffer from a low sense of concentration when you grieve. It is normal to see yourself facing the challenge of not remembering a task you should execute or discovering that you are lost while speaking with someone; there is something about negative emotion. An overwhelming swirl can characterize it. With this, you will find it difficult to focus – but do not be dismayed.

You are not in this alone. Most bereaved individuals experience similar situations. So, you should recognize the naturally occurring challenge and not harshly judge yourself for being preoccupied, confused, and dazed. I would advise you to be gentle with yourself and believe you will get through the stage. Factually, you will gain nothing by hurting and beating yourself up emotionally just because you are being human and normal.

Based on how your loved ones want to make you get over your grief, they would try as much as possible not to speak of anything that can trigger a negative feeling. This is right because many grievers will find it upsetting. Notwithstanding, there is nothing wrong with you telling them that it is all right for them to mention the name you enjoy hearing and any stories they may want to tell. This can help with quick recovery as you begin, over time, to see the whole situation as a typical challenge that life can push on anyone.

Do you get upset when people tell you that they know or understand how you feel or say it is important that you get over your situation? Well, this is not strange but normal. If the truth must be told, they speak out of their personal experience of loss but fail to understand that loss is personal. Irrespective of what you might have lost – each person's feelings and grief are their own. It is wrong for you to compare other people's circumstances with yours; emotional loss always leaves an indelible mark on the mind. You will continue to remember it throughout your lifetime.

Nonetheless, the opportunity is given to you to learn to cope with it and thrive. You may hear most grievers say that grief takes time, and that time heals all wounds. As far as your recovery from loss is concerned, time is never a factor. Time will always be there, and living through it will make the emotional pain become part of you – you will become used to it. But the actions you take towards moving on into a better future during this time are what matter.

Reconstruction and working through phases describe the period following a traumatic event or experience. This period is often characterized by healing, rebuilding, and re-establishing a sense of normalcy. During this period, individuals may experience various emotions, including grief, anger, fear, and confusion. It is essential to recognize that this time is necessary for individuals to process their emotions and experiences and begin moving forward.

As long as you continue to live, you will experience something that will bring into memory someone or something you have lost. Seeing this, you may feel sad and begin to think of what you could have done to avert such a tragedy or what you wish to have been different or better. However, this agony that fills your heart means nothing but the fact that there are still areas that are not well-addressed, which you need to take a bold step to deal with. Yes, it is evident that you miss the physical presence of what you have lost, but you can help yourself by easing the emotional pain that stops you from enjoying good memories.

Normally, you may grieve the loss you are experiencing when you lose a person, relationship, animal, or situation that is precious to you. Just like President Biden, you too can adopt an effective and healthy coping mechanism to deal with your pain in time, irrespective of the cause of your grief. Doing this, you will marvel at how your sadness will be eased, how you will come to an understanding of your condition, find new meaning to your existence, and move on to fulfill your purpose in life.

As you already know, in your life. When the loss is enormous, there is a high tendency that it will impact your life and even leave you questioning your sanity. During this situation, you may begin to see tasks that you once found simple to be exceedingly challenging. You may begin to be touched on an emotional level by both what people around you do and what they do not do.

Yes, you may take this personally and attack them far beyond their actions and inactions. Nonetheless, you must understand that it is normal to have these feelings and react in such ways. It is essential to recognize that this process may take time and that being patient and kind to oneself is crucial. It is also essential to recognize that moving forward and creating a new sense of purpose and meaning in life is possible.

The Stages of Your Grief

While experiencing grief, one of the crucial factors you

must bear in mind is to recognize where you are in the process and know when to ask for help. As you already know, grief is a reaction that could be experienced anytime reality becomes different from what you hoped for, wanted, or expected. For example, suppose you're experiencing traumatic and persistent grief; you will have to cycle through some stages of grief, which is the attempt to give change a chance and protect your emotional well-being while moving toward a new and pleasant reality. With your knowledge of these stages of grief and the best way you can experience them, you stand a chance of boosting your self-compassion and understanding. Reconstruction and working through the phase are integral to the healing process following a traumatic event or experience. Also, you will be able to know your needs and work toward meeting them.

The First Stage: Denial

The first step in the reconstruction and working through phase is recognizing the trauma and its effects. This includes acknowledging the trauma's physical, emotional, and psychological effects. It is important to recognize that the trauma may have had a lasting impact on the individual and that it is crucial to take the time to process these effects. The typical first stage of grief when your emotions are highly profound is denial. This is a stage that can help you survive your loss. It is also a stage when life makes no sense to you and happens to be overwhelming and meaningless. Here, you will go numb and find yourself in a state of shock. You will ask questions about how you can move on and why you need to move on. You will handle each day with care and do your best to live through it. Shock and denial are effective coping mechanisms that can help boost your chance of survival by making you work through your feelings of grief with ease.

Denial is a unique system through which you can let in only what you can handle. You will have to see the reality of your loss the way it is, accept it, and begin to ask yourself several questions. With this, you unconsciously go through the healing process and gain strength. Then, denial and shock will start to fade as you move on.

The Second Stage: Anger

The next step is to begin to rebuild. This includes coping with the trauma, seeking professional help, engaging in self-care activities, and connecting with supportive people. It is essential to recognize that rebuilding can take time, and one must be patient and kind during this process. For your healing process, anger is a vital stage. At this level, you will have to feel the anger that will appear forever. However, the anger will dissipate with time as you continue to feel it truly, leading to your healing. Although anger is generally seen as a negative emotion, it could sometimes be a strength and can serve as a tentative structure to the nothingness of losing someone or something. The moment you begin to grieve, you will feel lost and detached from everything around you. You will feel the rage taking over you and begin to get angry unnecessarily at some people. This anger will stand as a connection between you and them. Rather than holding onto nothing, the strength you get through anger is okay and will make you feel better.

The Third Stage: Bargaining

Everyone will do anything possible to stop the occurrence of a tragedy hitting a loved one. For instance, President Biden would have begged and bargained with God that if He could just save his wife and children, he would do something significant in exchange. It is possible that bargaining may appear as a tentative truce after a loss. You can say something like: if you could take your time to help the needy, you could wake up and see that the loss was just a dream. This is where you become trapped and begin using statements such as "what if" and "if only"; you will passionately desire to see the restoration of your loved ones and life returning to what it was.

The main thing that will occupy your mind will be the desire to go back in time to stop the crash from happening, recognize the sickness sooner, or find the tumor faster. In addition, bargaining and guilt are close companions. The more you think about what you could do if only you could be provided with a different opportunity, can make you start to find fault in yourself. In fact, you may even decide to make a deal with your pain; it is normal.

You will be highly interested in doing whatever it may require avoiding feeling the pain that comes with the loss. With this, you attempt to stay in the past and bargain your way out of your emotional crisis. Most times, people tend to see the stages last for months or weeks. However, that is only sometimes the reality. They sometimes are responses that can be experienced for hours or minutes as you move in and out of one another. You cannot get in and out of each stage in a linear fashion; after feeling one, you flip to another and then return to the first one.

The Fourth Stage: Depression

The moment you are done making a deal with your pain, your focus will shift to your present. What then will happen? This is when you begin to have empty feelings and get more overwhelmed by the grief in your life; this is called the depression stage. It is a more profound level where you start to have a feeling that you may think will last for the rest of your lifetime.

It would help if you did not confuse this depression with a mental health challenge – yes, they are different. This depression is just a mere reaction to your significant loss. At this stage, you begin to withdraw gradually from what makes your life meaningful and journey down the road of intense sadness, thinking there is no actual point in moving on. Feeling depressed after suffering from a loss is usually perceived to be unnatural. It is nothing but something you must pull yourself out of and a state you need to deal with. Here, you must ask yourself whether your present condition is depressing.

Undoubtedly, losing someone or something you love can be highly depressing, so it is not abnormal for your reaction to such a situation to be depression. However, it will be unusual for you not to feel depressed after losing a loved one. After allowing the feeling of loss to take a full grip on your soul, you will find it comprehensively depressing to realize that your loved one failed to escape the tragic occurrence. As you already know, grief is one of the active processes toward healing; therefore, getting depressed will be vital.

The Fifth Stage: Acceptance

I will be going deeper into the concept of acceptance in the fifth chapter of this book, but before then, let me tell you a little about it as a stage of your grief. First, you should not confuse acceptance with being a notion that relates to the fact that you are perfectly "okay" or "all right" with what you have faced in life. Yes, it is different. Many grievers will not feel all right or okay about losing someone or something they love. So, what is the notion of "acceptance" all about?

Acceptance is a stage where you admit the reality that the person or thing you have lost is gone physically and realize that the new reality is permanent. This new reality is one you will not like or see as okay, but you will have to accept it and do what you can to live with it. Yes, you will see reality as a norm; you have no option but to learn to live. Here is where life presents you with a new world where your loved ones are not, and you must live therein.

Nonetheless, if you refuse to live in this world and accept the new norm, you may initially intend to maintain your normal life as you had before you lost your loved ones. But, after some time, acceptance will start to set in as you will notice that you will not be able to keep your past as it was. The reality is that the past has been altered forever, and you must now readjust your life and learn to live it the way it is. You must now focus on reorganizing roles and re-assigning them to people around you, or you may even decide to take them on yourself.

Acceptance is a vital step when grieving. With it, you will have more good days. Nevertheless, as you continue to live everyday life and bask in the pleasure of the present, the guilt of living happily without your loved ones may set in – you may start to think you are betraying them. Understandably, your loved ones are irreplaceable, but you cannot deny yourself the opportunity to build meaningful relationships. Make new connections, and establish new interdependence, which is good for well-being. I am not saying you should restrict your feelings; you should never do. Instead, you need to pay close attention to what you need, become optimistic about life, do your best to move on, embrace the change that comes with life, grow your potential, and evolve. After losing a lovely wife and two children, President Biden expressed that he followed a specific way that helped him get through his grief. This way, he developed a sense of purpose and took on a responsibility that he thought would make Neilia, his lost wife, and his children proud of him. He said his intention then was to make people optimistic that they could find their way through grief via purpose. Like President Biden, you can do well by reaching out to others to offer any assistance you can provide and investing in interpersonal and intrapersonal relationships. With this, you can be guaranteed a new everyday life. Nevertheless, this will never be possible if you fail to give grief its own time.

Emotional Reconstruction: Feel Sense of Control Over Your Life Again

The reconstruction phase is also one of the stages of grief that I want you to know. As a process, grieving is not always about feeling overwhelmed and stressed. When you reach the reconstruction and work through a stage of grief, you will start to get past the aftermath of losing someone or something you love. Although some emotional experts may not list this phase as one of the stages of grief, it is as much a part of the grieving process.

Nevertheless, the emotional reconstruction stage takes a unique way; it is a stage where you start feeling a sense of control over your existence.

This phase is a stage of reality; after going through the pain of losing someone or something, you may begin to see several things not matter anymore. But these unimportant things will start to matter to you again at this phase. For me, after counting a lot of things as insignificant, when I got to the reconstruction stage, I started to see these things as necessary again. Taking care of my family has always been a priority in life; after the death of my daughter and the trauma I had to go through due to divorce, I began to see relationships and moving forward in life as something that did not really matter. But later, I realized I needed to handle the relationship with my other children better and work toward my future and career goals. With this, I passionately believed that I would move forward.

Emotional reconstruction is what you need when you feel you are walking into uncertainty. At this point in your life, you will feel extreme sadness as there is no way out or light at the end of the tunnel. But the moment you rebuild yourself emotionally, you will start to regain security and begin to express a notable change in life.

As you move on with your life and become more active and functional, you will have your mind improved. But you need to understand that it is not that you will not be feeling sad, angry, depressed, or guilty anymore – it is a time that you will begin to see everything for the way they are and work on how you can start to live a normal life again.

At this stage in your emotional crisis journey, you will develop the ability to look for ways to embrace change and move along. You may focus on how to deal with your financial challenge and other pragmatic problems; doing this effectively will help you return to a state of better normalcy. With emotional reconstruction, the quality of your life will be improved. You will find yourself in some healthier relationships, establish a better relationship with yourself, your emotional suffering will be eased, your assertiveness will be boosted, you will develop higher self-esteem, your self-knowledge will increase, and you will develop better emotional management skills.

Emotional reconstruction can be a challenging task that may require several resources. Nevertheless, it is worth it. You may want to ask for the best and the most effective methods you can employ to work through grief and loss; this is an excellent question to ask, and the correct answer to it will help you take good advantage of the stage before getting to the acceptance phase.

There is no right time but now to decide to put your life in a better position. Emotional reconstruction is a process of giving the new foundation of your life a preferred design and structure. Here, you need to make up your mind to prune or transform everything you know that is a source of your pain. The time to feel hurt is over; you are taking charge. This includes finding ways to move forward and create a new sense of purpose and meaning in life. This may include engaging in activities that bring joy and fulfillment, such as hobbies, volunteering, or meaningful relationships.

A Good Understanding of Yourself

Comprehending who you are intensively, or knowing yourself better, is a typical action that anyone who wants to reach a great height in life must take. This method will work effectively for you while going through the grief of loss to better your life. Here, you will have to analyze the current situation in your life comprehensively. It would help if you made an incredible effort to think deeply, to come up with the things that are hurting you.

It will be better to find a quiet place to sit and give your recent crisis events an excellent analysis to position yourself for transformation, ideally.

A good understanding of yourself is essential for leading a successful and fulfilling life. It involves knowing strengths and weaknesses, understanding values and beliefs, and being aware of emotions and how they affect behavior. It also involves understanding how past experiences have shaped who you are today and how they may influence the future. Understanding yourself can help you make better decisions and set realistic goals. It can also help build better relationships with others and better communicate needs and feelings.

Additionally, it can help manage stress and difficult emotions, as it will be better able to recognize and address the underlying causes of distress. Developing a good understanding can be a lifelong process. It involves taking the time to reflect on experiences, values, and beliefs and to explore emotions and behavior. It also involves being open to learning new things about yourself and being willing to make changes when necessary. One way to start developing a better understanding is to keep a journal. Writing down thoughts and feelings can help you gain insight into your behavior and emotions.

Furthermore, talking to a trusted friend or family member can help gain a better understanding as it may be able to provide an outside perspective. Finally, it is essential to remember that having a good understanding is not about perfection. It is about being honest and accepting who you are. It is also about being open to learning, growing, and making changes when necessary.

You will analyze the failures and victories you have experienced so far. However, you should expect to avoid seeing an immediate result because the process is gradual; the moment you identify and know the noteworthy events in your life, you will surely gain a better knowledge of who you are. With this, insight will come into whatever you have in mind to do.

Assertiveness

Another crucial step you need to take is becoming assertive. This implies that you must show what you are going through in your life, regardless of how difficult it could be. Assertiveness is an important communication skill that can help you express needs effectively and stand up for your rights in a respectful way. It involves expressing thoughts, feelings and needs directly and honestly while respecting the rights, opinions, and beliefs without infringing the rights of others. Assertiveness can help build better relationships, resolve conflicts, and make decisions in the best interest. When it comes to being assertive, it is essential to be aware of body language and tone of voice. Make sure your body language is an open and inviting tone of voice that is confident and clear. It is also essential to be aware of words and how they might be interpreted. Avoid using aggressive or passive-aggressive language; instead, focus on using "I" statements that clearly express your thoughts and feelings.

Most times, you will find it arduous to tell your boss or a loved one "NO," even if it is essential to say that to defend your right and be able to negotiate and compromise when appropriate. But when it comes to reconstruction and working through, you must be assertive; this is a wonderful way to see yourself as autonomous and capable of responsibility. Finally, it's vital to practice assertiveness in a variety of situations. This can help you become more comfortable with expressing yourself in a direct and respectful manner. It can also help you become more confident in standing up for yourself and your beliefs. With assertiveness, a sense of control that has already been affected by your negative emotions can be regained.

Self-esteem

Negative emotions such as sadness, anger, depression, and guilt can affect the love you have for yourself, thereby influencing your self-esteem. By self-esteem, I mean the standard evaluation of your true worth. You may wonder what self-esteem has to do with reconstruction and working through it. To generate positive emotions, it is more likely that people will do good to those that do the same to them. Self-esteem is a term used to describe the belief in one's abilities and worth. It is confidence and pride in oneself and one's accomplishments. Self-esteem is integral to personal growth and development and is essential for a healthy and prosperous life. It is not something given but must be cultivated and nurtured within yourself. It results from positive experiences, such as success in school or work or favorable relationships with family and friends.

Moreover, it is also the result of positive self-talk and self-affirmation, which is important because it helps to feel good and on accomplishments. It gives the confidence to take risks, try new things, achieve goals that would, and make decisions in the best interest. Self-esteem is crucial because it helps to cope with difficult situations and to handle stress. Healthy self-esteem can better handle criticism and failure and learn from mistakes, thus better recognizing strengths and weaknesses and using them to your advantage. Finally, self-esteem is important because it helps build strong relationships. Having better communication needs and feelings and building trust and respect with others can lead to accepting and appreciating the differences in others.

Due to this, there is a higher tendency that if you treat yourself well, you will be moved to treat well those who are treating you well. You should not see this as confusing – this has a circular effect, and the idea is that you will always want to take care of yourself by loving and building yourself.

Change

Change is a beautiful thing, and therefore you need to embrace it. Emotional reconstruction can only be discussed by explaining how it can bring about external and internal changes. Change is an inevitable part of life. It is something that we all must face and learn to accept. Change can be both positive and negative and can come in many forms. It can be in our environment, relationships, jobs, health, or even beliefs. Change can be sudden, unexpected, or gradual and planned. No matter what form it takes, change can be challenging to adjust to and can cause stress and anxiety. It is important to remember that change is a natural part of life and that it can bring about new opportunities and experiences. It is also important to recognize that change can be difficult and that it is okay to feel overwhelmed or scared. It is essential to take the time to process the change and to find ways to cope with it. One way to cope with change is to focus on its positive aspects of it. Thinking about how the change can bring about new opportunities and experiences can be helpful. It can also be beneficial to talk to friends and family about the change and to get their support. It can also be beneficial to practice self-care and take time to relax and process the change. Change can be difficult, but it can also be a positive experience. It is important to remember that change is a natural part of life and that it can bring about new opportunities and experiences. It is also essential to be flexible and open-minded and to find ways to cope with the change. With the right attitude and support, change can be a positive experience. Your focus should be on how you can transform your life. Before this, you may return to a position of balance by making necessary adjustments to return to your pre-crisis state.

Chapter Four

Self-Motivation: Get Over the Bad Experiences

Mariska Hargitay, popularly known as Oliver Benson, is one of the celebrities whose life experiences have inspired millions of people in distinct parts of the world. However, her life was not as radiant as you can see today; it could be said that she was built out of tragic events that occurred to her at the early stage of her life. Hargitay's story revealed that when she was just three years old, her mother – Jayne Mansfield, an iconic screen actor thirty-four-year-old – died in a car crash while Mariska was asleep in the backseat of the vehicle. Hargitay would constantly be reminded of this traumatic event by the scar on the side of her head. While speaking with *Redbook* in 2009, expressing her view on life, Hargitay showed that the tragic incident changed her life; she said it was a scar on her soul to have lost her mother at such an early age. Nonetheless, she revealed that she had the feeling that the unfortunate event contributed immensely to what she had become. Hargitay said she was not ignorant of life's journey and had to go through that to be where she found herself today.

Has life ever turned so hard against you to the extent that it becomes your everyday routine to cry and feel down? Are you wondering why life becomes so hard that you think there is nothing you can do to deal with it? I want you to know that you are not alone – several people journeyed down the same road as you and transformed positively. If they could do it, you, too, can shift your life for the better after getting over the bad experiences you might have had.

One of the reasons why life is hard on you is that you are a creature of desires, emotions, fears, and needs. It is common to see people utilize spiritual or religious explanations when faced with a specific challenge, such as the loss of a loved one or job. They think through this they can see hope that will help calm them. But when such events happen to someone else, they tend to make a differentiation, seeking what exactly makes them safe. For these reasons, they get the protection they need. Notwithstanding, they may need to – at a certain point – accept the fact that no one is truly safe from life.

Tragedy can hit anyone; that's the truth. This is because of our susceptibility to injury, disease, and negative emotions. So, you can feel so overwhelmed due to the loss of someone close to you, suffering a significant health challenge, the end of an intimate friendship or relationship, actions causing distress to someone else or considerable pain, something ending like a business project/venture or job, and a major failure that leads to a significant economic loss. When any of these eventually happens, how do you find motivation? It usually becomes difficult to find the strength to move on, not to talk of getting the willpower to shift your life for the better after suffering from life's catastrophe. You usually have sleepless nights due to the pain and headache that follow misfortune; you may even see it as impossible to get the courage to get your life back on track after a loss.

Due to how grief is an inevitable part of life, it is, therefore, precious if you know how to take advantage of the misfortune to become a better person.

My grief came when I lost a daughter and a relationship of many years; my experience made me understand that people see grief differently. Some individuals see it as a complex emotional crisis that is difficult to get through, while others see it as a chance to revitalize old relationships. But personally, my grief allowed me to think about what really mattered most in my life. When life is going smoothly, and fortune is there smiling, we sometimes become carried away by our daily events and disconnected from what is truly crucial to our existence. With my misfortune, I was able to remind myself that I had no idea when people would grieve about me. So, it was vital to pick my life up from where I had dropped it and do the best I could while still breathing. Yes, life will always happen repeatedly, but I have always made up my mind to get back on track and reprioritize my attention to improving my life. So, when it is my time to go, I will have no regret.

Grief and Lack of Motivation

Yes, lack of motivation and grief are tied. When you're going through the grieving phase, there is a high tendency for you will become downright apathetic, lethargic, and sluggish. Even though you can easily pass the blame for not being functional to a lack of motivation, you should understand that these negative feelings during your grieving process are not the result of your failure.

The American Brain Foundation's research discovered that stressful events or traumatic situations – including the loss of loved ones – will evoke a survival reaction from your body; this reaction can make you feel unmotivated and unable to focus. You need to know that the manifestation of grief is natural, and you should not be blamed for not feeling motivated to get things done.

Grief and lack of motivation can be challenging to manage, and it is a natural response to a loss, for it can be overwhelming and debilitating. It can cause a person to feel disconnected from the world and unable to find the motivation to do anything. This can be especially difficult if the person is also dealing with a lack of motivation. When someone is grieving, it is essential to remember that it is a normal and natural response to loss. It is crucial to allow yourself to feel the emotions that come with grief and not try to push them away. Be gentle with and do not expect too much from yourself; taking time to process emotions and care for yourself is okay. When it comes to a lack of motivation, it is essential to remember that it is a common symptom of grief. Being patient and finding activities to help one feel more motivated is important. This could include walking, listening to music, or engaging in enjoyable activities. It is also essential to reach out for help if need be. Talking to a therapist or a trusted friend can be a great way to process emotions and find ways to cope with grief and lack of motivation. It is also important to remember that grief and lack of motivation are not permanent states and that, with time and effort, you can find ways to cope and move forward.

Finding motivation can be incredibly challenging after losing something or someone you love. Most times, you may be overwhelmed by the negative emotions, making it uneasy to find your way out of the pain that the loss has caused you; even the thrill of engaging yourself in anything meaningful could be gone. Yes, it is never strange to feel pessimistic, or that joy and happiness are no longer for you in this world. Moreover, the grief of losing someone or something you love can affect your motivation by leading to emotional numbness, hopelessness, loss of interest in daily life, absence of energy to get things done, and feelings of physical and emotional exhaustion.

While it is true that the deed has already been done and there is nothing you can do to return to where you were, you still have the chance to heal from your suffering and pain and live your life in a better way again. But you will need to work on how you can give your life new meaning by working through and coping with grief.

The truth is that you will only be stressing yourself unnecessarily, making healing more difficult, if you keep putting the blame on yourself. In this case, you must understand that grieving usually takes some time. Therefore, it is understandable that you may feel indifferent about life today, tomorrow, and more days to come. Still, suppose you concentrate on caring for yourself and giving grief a chance to have its moment. In that case, you will develop a good feeling and, finally, get over the unpleasant experience.

Grief and Positive Outcome

In several ways, it has been confirmed that you will not see grief unfold in neat stages but that the oscillation between several mental processes and states distinctly characterizes it. One of the several important things that have been said about grief is that coping with bereavement can give you room for significant positive results; this is called posttraumatic growth.

Posttraumatic growth occurs when you experience significant life challenges, great suffering, and psychological distress. But you should know that not everyone faced with substantial stressors will experience this growth; this is because it is a process that involves indispensable steps that need to be observed. Failure to give credence to these steps will indeed amount to adverse outcomes rather than positive ones.

Five different areas must be experienced to actualize posttraumatic growth; self-perception is one of the top areas. When you experience loss can make you start seeing yourself as more confident and stronger; this is why you will hear people say that, due to how they have been through the worst, they are now capable of dealing with any situation that may present itself.

However, it is essential to remember that grief can also have positive outcomes. One positive outcome of grief is that it can help you appreciate life more. Experiencing a loss can be a reminder of how precious life is and how important it is to make the most of time.

Grief can also help us appreciate our relationships with others and recognize the importance of spending time with those we love. Experiencing a loss can be a challenging experience, but it can also be an opportunity to learn and grow. You are learning to be more resilient, cope with difficult emotions, and be more compassionate and understanding of others who are going through similar experiences with grief. It can also help us to connect with others when experiencing a loss; it can be comforting to know that you are not alone. Finding support and comfort in the people around you and knowing that others have gone through similar experiences could give you solace. Finally, grief can help to find meaning in life. Experiencing a loss can remind us how important it is to live a meaningful life. Use grief as an opportunity to reflect on lives and to find purpose in the experience.

Why You Can Be a Better Person Through Grief

You can look at grief differently, but the ideal perspective I want you to have is how you use it as a catalyst to grow yourself and improve your life's quality.

If you want to know why grief can make you a better person, the first reason I will tell you is that grief will teach you valuable lessons. It is commonly said that life is the best teacher. Yes, that is true because we will continue learning until we die. In the case of grief, it can come in different forms, such as financial or relationship loss. If you grieved because you faced terrible challenges in any of these areas in the past, you could be aroused to do things better when a comparable situation shows itself again. This is because you have gained a new level of awareness and experience; these will equip and prepare you to be wise in your decision-making to create a better and desirable positive outcome.

After the death of J.K Rowling's mother, she moved to Portugal to work as an English teacher. While in Portugal, she married and gave birth to a daughter after she suffered from a miscarriage. As life would have it, her marriage ended up broken. After that, she had to return to the UK with nothing and was extremely depressed. While talking with Britain's *Sunday*, Rowling said she thought about suicide because her life was miserable. While in the United Kingdom, she got a teaching job in Edinburgh, Scotland, where the idea of drafting the popular book series *Harry Potter* came to her mind. After completing the book, she reached out to several publishers. Unfortunately, the book was rejected many times. However, Rowling did not relent since she knew that life could sometimes be challenging. Finally, the opportunity came, and a deal was made with her for *Harry Potter and the Sorcerer's Stone.*

Grief will make you see your relationships differently.

As you continue to live among people you love, something dramatic may involve other people. When this happens, a new opportunity will be presented for you to evaluate if your relationships are holding you down from moving forward or positively influencing your life. You will see people coming in and going out of your life, but you have to decide which individuals are appropriate to be in your circle.

The Popular American billionaire entrepreneur, media proprietor, and television personality Mark Cuban once faced the terrible side of life. He once worked at a company that was into PC software sales while living with five of his friends in a three-bedroom apartment. He struggled as a young man and was even fired from his workplace. His setback taught him a great lesson, and he decided to set up his own business and become his boss. Cuban writes in his book *How to Win at the Sport of Business* that he described his former boss as his mentor, even if it was the other way around. He said that today, he could think about what the boss did, and from what he had learned, he would do the opposite. Cuban wrote to young professionals to keep learning, grinding, and not stop loving their lives.

Grief will make you question your actions.

One of the best accountability questions you can ask yourself is, "let's assume someone tells me that all I have left to live is six months. Will I continue doing things the way I have been doing them?" his question is never about if what you are doing is wrong or right but about gaining awareness of the things that matter most to you. The famous scientist Stephen Hawking, not long after his twenty-first birthday, was diagnosed with a terrible disease called Amyotrophic Lateral Sclerosis (ALS); this sickness caused him to have no control over most of the muscles in his body. The doctor told him that he had only two to four years to live. Hawking never let this stop him from growing but decided to focus all his energy on learning everything he could within the fleeting time he had left. Before he was diagnosed with this sickness, Hawking claimed he was living his life in boredom; therefore, he attributed his exceptionality to his misfortune. The funniest part is that this man lived until he was seventy-six years old, making an incredible impact on science through his work. This shows that grief can push you to question where you have always been and challenge you to be the better version of yourself.

Grief can often lead to questioning your actions; when grieving, there are questions about decisions, relationships, and life choices. You may wonder if there could have done something differently or if there could have prevented the loss. You may also question strength and resilience and whether you can get through this difficult time and wonder if your beliefs are still valid or if they have been shaken. It is questioning your ability to cope with the pain and suffering that comes with grief. Remember that it is a necessary part of healing; thus, it is okay to have only some answers.

Grief will teach you how to appreciate life more.

Your understanding of life – that you will only be here for a limited period – is strong enough to motivate you. Seeing life as a gift that needs to be more appreciated can change your perspective about your present state to strive toward your passion and to live a life of mission and purpose. With this, you can experience happiness from time to time. Helen Keller, the famous American author, lecturer, political activist, and disability rights advocate, said in one of her unique quotes that on several occasions, a door of happiness would close. Still, when this happens, another door of happiness will open. She wrote that most times, people focus on the closed door so long that they fail to see the new one that has been opened.

Even though Keller was an activist, author, and lecturer, she was both blind and deaf. However, she did not allow her disability to stop her from achieving remarkable things. Keller worked so hard, and she became the first blind-deaf person to be given a Bachelor of Arts degree. In 1971, she got inducted into the Alabama Women's Hall of Fame. By studying the inspirational life of this woman, no adversity is too immense for you to overcome to live a meaningful life. Looking at Keller's situation, no one would have criticized her if she had given up. Still, she saw life as a gift despite her challenges and lived beyond her limitations to become one of the most inspirational people in the world.

Grief will make you let go of insignificant things.

While everything is going so well in your life, you may find it relatively easy to get involved in things that are not important. Nonetheless, if the table turns and a significant crisis occurs, you will start to see that trivial thing amount to nothing. Grief can cause us to let go of things that we may have previously held onto for various reasons, such as fear, guilt, or even a sense of obligation and even out of comfort or familiarity. You may have held onto certain things because they were a part of your identity or past. The realization is that these things no longer serve the purpose and that it is time to let them go, for they bring pain. Moreover, these things are no longer part of the present or future; they are no longer important; it is time to move on. By letting go of these things, you can begin to move forward and focus on what is truly essential.

Therefore, ask yourself what you want to experience or create in each moment of your life. The idea is that the more you concentrate on essential things, the less attention you will give to things of no significance.

Grief will move you to contribute to another people's life.

Pain is what no one wishes for. After going through your grim times, battling with sadness, anger, guilt, and depression, you may be moved to provide needed help to others who are going through similar challenges. This is quite common in present-day society, as many individuals set up different non-profit organizations (NGOs) to help people escape or escape the grief they once experienced. The good thing about this is that when you stretch out your hand to help others, you will experience joy and fulfillment. You may have heard the inspiring story of Dashrath Manjhi, popularly known as the Mountain Man. His poor environment led to the death of his wife. After the woman was injured, the nearest doctor who could help her could not come early due to the poor road system, leading to the tragic event. This experience triggered Manjhi's passion for making a new roadway to make Gehlaur Village more accessible; the result of his effort was a 110-meter-long path carved into a ridge of hills. Manjhi only used a chisel and a hammer in building this road and got the job done between 1960 and 1982 – taking him twenty-two years to finish. He lived a fulfilled life because the road he made cut the previous distance to the village from thirty-four miles to nine miles.

Grief will make you see your experiences and memories as valuable.

You should not be astonished if you hear that grief can effectively make you remember and reflect on things, including your previous firsthand experiences or those you had with others. Regardless of the source of the incidents, as much as you were in the picture, they are powerful enough to make you the person you are designed to be; your memories have the tendency to shift your life for the better.

MOVING ALONG

When grieving, it reminds you of the importance of the people, places, and things that have been lost. The joys and sorrows that were shared with them and the impact that they have had on someone's life would remain valuable; memories will be cherished forever. It is also an eye-opener to appreciate the moments with the people and things still in life. Furthermore, it is a realization of how precious and fragile life is and how quickly it can be taken away. Cherish the moments with loved ones, make the most of the time, appreciate the little things in life, and take nothing for granted, for life is uncertain. The lessons learned and the growth experienced were what you gained from the strength, resilience, and courage you found to keep going. Most important is the beauty of the experience because of the love that you have shared.

Regain Motivation: Ways to Get Over Bad Experiences

Rather than sitting down all day getting beaten by your negative emotions or embracing a lack of excitement about waking up in the morning, you can channel your energy toward making meaning in grief. Grief can sap your interest in everything you once found joy in and make you think all hope is lost; even when it is totally ignored, it can pose a risk of developing severe challenges, such as depression and chronic grief.

The moment you begin to develop the passion for getting over your bad experiences and shifting your life for the better, the next thing you should work toward is regaining the lost motivation; doing this will help you with a healthy grief recovery. So, what practical ways can you regain some of your lost inspiration?

Regaining motivation after a bad experience can be challenging to overcome, but it can be possible to learn from them and move on. Some tips to help restore motivation and overcome bad experiences:

1. Acknowledge feelings and take the time to process them. Allowing you to feel the emotions that come with the experience and not be afraid to talk about them with someone you trust would help unload the weight on your chest.

2. Taking a break from the situation can help you gain perspective and distance yourself from experience; it can help to gain clarity and move on.

3. Focus on the positives; sometimes, it can be easy to focus on the negatives of a bad experience. Instead, think about the experience and how it can help in the future.

4. Set goals to help regain motivation and focus on the future. Make sure goals are achievable and plan to reach them.

5. Take care of yourself; it is essential for regaining motivation. Get enough sleep, eat healthily, and exercise regularly.

6. Reach for help; if struggling to regain motivation, be bold and reach out for help. Talking to a friend, family member, or professional can help you.

Obey the Law of Time

Grief is not a process you should expect to go away momentarily; you cannot compare your grief journey with that of others. Everyone must follow their unconventional path and honor the timeline – and since it is basically about the experience, there is no wrong or right way to oversee it. I want you to know that healing from grief usually takes time. You can't put yourself in a rushing mode, trying to reach the finish line on time; there might not be a finish line when it comes to grieving.

Obeying the law of time is essential for living a balanced and productive life by using time wisely and not wasting it. Prioritizing tasks and activities and focusing on the most important ones is a must. Be mindful of how to spend time and ensure that it is well-spent on activities that are not beneficial and spending on specific activities, thus not overdoing it. Time is a precious resource, and it is essential to use it wisely, like using social media but should not neglect relationships or time spent on hobbies and not neglecting work. In addition, be aware of how much time you spend on relationships and ensure to pay attention to your own needs. Following this law ensures living a balanced and productive life.

What you need to keep in mind is that the suffering and pain you feel will dissipate as time goes on, which is the appropriate time for you to use your emotional energy in a positive way for yourself while also strengthening other relationships. There are days when you will feel an incredible improvement, while some days will come when your grief totally engulfs you.

Notwithstanding, what could be the average period for you to get healed? You may need about twelve months to recover from normal grief; this average period is a good indicator. Nonetheless, you may have to deal with grief for many years if you are dealing with a complicated one. Besides, some people will continue to face it for the rest of their life. Since grieving can be painful, you may need to give yourself the time to express your grief and heal.

Get a Wish List

There are several things you may need help to do at a specific time; before this time comes, you could make a wish list that contains all these things you wish you could do. These may be things you want to accomplish before death, illness, or advanced age sets in.

You should find it motivating to write down the list. With this, you can regain clarity and focus on how you live your life and identify a new thing you can do that can bring meaning into your existence. First, you need to arrange the items on the list according to their order of priority and importance, and then you should keep the list somewhere. Then, after a few months or weeks, you will remember and try to check from where you may have hidden it.

A wish list before death is a great way to ensure that your last wishes are fulfilled and that your loved ones are taken care of. It can be difficult and emotional, but it is important to ensure that your wishes are known and respected.

When creating a wish list before death, the first thing to consider is to make sure that your wishes are legally binding. This means that you should consult with a lawyer to ensure that your wishes are properly documented and that they will be respected. The next step is to make sure that your wishes are communicated to your loved ones. This can be done through a will, a trust, or a letter. It is important to make sure that your wishes are clearly stated and that your loved ones understand them. You should also ensure that your wishes are regularly updated, as your wishes may change over time. When creating a wish list before death, it is important to consider your financial situation. You should make sure that your wishes are financially feasible and that your loved ones will be able to carry out your wishes. You should also consider any debts or assets that you may have and ensure they are taken care of. Finally, you should consider any charitable donations that you may want to make. This can be a great way to ensure that your legacy lives on. Consider any special requests that you may have, such as a specific funeral service or a special memorial.

Besides, you may need to manage one thing at a time. Most of your emotional energy should be reserved for things of greater importance on your list – and you should never forget how important you are. This is why you need to add yourself to your to-do list of what you give ultimate attention to.

Take a Trip Alone

It would help if you went through grief alone; it is an emotional battle. So, the help people can do will be to support you, give you opportunities to talk about your loss, keep encouraging you, help you plan, and perhaps take a day off to spend it with you. But when it comes to pain and suffering, you need to experience it all by yourself; therefore, you need to go somewhere alone without disturbance. With this, you can grant your soul the healing it needs. The thought may come to your mind that your grieving period is not the appropriate time to go on a trip alone; regardless of what you may think, going somewhere alone comes with several potential benefits after losing someone or something you love.

Taking a trip alone when in grief can be a great way to take a break from the pain and sadness of your loss. It can be a time to reflect, heal, and find peace. It can also be a time to explore new places, meet new people, gain a new perspective on life, and find joy in the present moment. When planning a trip alone, it is crucial to consider emotional and physical needs. Make sure to plan how to handle any difficult emotions that may arise. It is also essential to plan for your safety and security. Make sure you have a plan for where you will stay, how you will get around, and how you will stay in touch with family and friends. Once you have a plan in place, it is important to take the time to enjoy the journey. Make sure to get enough rest, eat healthy meals, and take time to relax. It is also essential to process grief and allow yourself to feel the emotions. With a small quantity of planning and self-care, it can be a rewarding and healing experience.

You should see this as an opportunity to bond with your loved one, reconnect with yourself, or leave your grief behind for a while.

When you are there with no one, you will be able to think clearly and deeply, which can help you rediscover your authentic self, clear your mind from negative thoughts, and refocus your emotional energies on how your life can shift for the better.

Find a New Hobby

You will find it challenging to think about anything other than what you lost when your loved one is gone. Your attention will solely be on them, to the extent that you can even be reminded of the individual by petty things. Therefore, you should give yourself room to process the misfortune before returning to normal life. Nevertheless, one of the coping mechanisms that can help you is finding a new hobby after suffering from the loss.

After the loss of a loved one, finding a new hobby that brings joy and purpose back into your life can be challenging. Searching for something that can fill the void can be difficult. However, finding something that can help you cope with the grief and provide a sense of comfort and joy is essential. One hobby that can be beneficial after suffering from losing a loved one is gardening. Gardening can be a great way to honor the memory of your loved one and to bring beauty and life back. Planting flowers, vegetables, or herbs can be a great way to bring peace and joy. Gardening can also be a great way to connect with nature and find solace in the beauty of the outdoors. Another hobby that can be beneficial after suffering from the loss of a loved one is art. Art can be a great way to express your emotions to find comfort in the creative process. Whether it is painting, drawing, sculpting, or any other art form, it can be a great way to express yourself and find joy in the creative process. Finally, another hobby that can be beneficial after suffering from losing a loved one is volunteering. Volunteering can be a great way to give back to the community and help others in need. It can also be a great way to honor the memory of a loved one and to find purpose in helping others. No matter what hobby you choose, it is essential to take your time and find something you genuinely enjoy. It is a great way to cope with grief and find purpose in life again.

With a hobby, you can get a brief interval of relief from your sorrow; this is because the hobby will healthily distract you from your suffering and pain and can even help you ease any negative feelings and other symptoms of grief.

Discover Your New Person

The pain usually will not leave you to be the same person you once were. Instead, it can motivate you to become a better person. This is why you need to take your time to know the new you. After the discovery, you will plan how you intend to live your life and how you want it to be from that moment onward.

Pain can be a reminder of mortality and the fragility of life. It is essential to cherish moments and strive to make the most of your life. Pain tests strength and resilience, and capacity to overcome adversity. Self-care and mental and physical health are of utmost importance, especially kindness and understanding towards yourself and others. It focuses on the importance of learning from mistakes, growing from experiences, being open to change, and embracing new opportunities.

The bitter truth is that your identity and role will change when you lose those you love. After losing a child, I discovered I wasn't the same person I used to be. A large part of me was no longer there. This was why I had to seek ways to reinvent myself while holding on tightly to the person I was before suffering from the loss.

Lean on Gratefulness

Finding reasons to be grateful is one of the best things you can do when grieving. Despite how terrible the event that has led to your grief is, you still have yourself and others around you to be grateful for. By being thankful for the gift of life, you will be able to live your life for the individual you have lost or for something that can change your life positively forever. In addition, since you are still living, you can decide to be better – not only for the sake of yourself but also for those who need a life they can look up to for inspiration or emotional support.

One crucial question you may need to ask yourself is what you can do while you are still alive and have more days to experience life. As I have already discussed, you can find a new hobby. You can also start habits, like contacting the family and friends you have always wanted to call daily, taking a walk in the morning to be thankful for a new day, or preparing a meal more often for yourself. These and other healthy habits can significantly motivate you to improve your life.

Turn Your Grief into Inspiration

Your focus should be on taking advantage of your grief and turning it into inspiration. Then, you can pursue a goal in life, which may be working toward becoming a better person (personal) or helping others to get to where they need to be (for your organization). I could remember a friend of mine, Catharine, who lost her mum to breast cancer; her grief motivated her to reach out to others and share information about the illness. She also donated generously to the community initiative and research centers; her motivation was to inspire people to have relevant information about the important things to her.

Grief is a normal and necessary part of life that is overwhelming and difficult to process. It is hard when feeling so much pain and sadness. However, it is possible to turn our grief into inspiration. One way to do this is to focus on the positive aspects of the situation. Instead of dwelling on the loss, try to remember the good times and the memories shared with the person or thing you are grieving. This can bring a sense of peace and comfort; importantly, cherishing the time with your loved ones brings back balance.

Another way to turn grief into inspiration is to take care of yourself and focus on well-being, be gentle, and allow yourself to feel the emotions that come with grief. It is not easy, but it would get less pain every passing day

Chapter Five

Acceptance

If you are still thinking about **how**, it's possible to cope with the feeling of grief and rebuild your life, you may want to learn from Wendy's story. In her article *Grief and Sympathy*, she used her life's story to show you can find joy after grief. Wendy wrote out of curiosity about how her husband, who could be seen as a wonderful man, would be taken away by death; She lost her husband to a malignant brain tumor. Then, six months after Wendy's husband was gone, she lost a breast due to cancer.

Wendy recounted that it was like hell on earth for her for five years. Within this period of losing a partner and a breast, she also lost her father and eight of her intimate friends. What a great challenge for one person! To face this situation, Wendy had to think deeply about life and decided she would not waste her energy asking rhetorical questions about the events. This is because she understood that life could be awful sometimes, and when such events occur, no one has control over them; there is no way anyone could have predicted or comprehended them.

Wendy accepted her fate and showed that the agony gave her much personal strength, increased her self-awareness, and boosted her ability to see the joy in life. Wendy concluded her write-ups by saying that even though it is unavoidable to escape life's challenges, you can choose not to let the challenges get you down. She expounded that joy is always available everywhere for you if only you can make it a mission to look closely, regardless of the most unimaginable grief you might have endured. She said that making it happen is feasible by trying your best to work your situation through.

Wendy has taught great lessons about the acceptance stage of grief and how attainable it is; this is a stage you should strive to reach after experiencing several negative emotions, such as denial, shock, anger, grief, regret, depression, and guilt. After a significant loss, finding acceptance is never an impossible process. If numerous people can reach this stage, you can as well. At this stage, your emotions, body, and mind will acknowledge that the event has happened and learn to live with the change by assimilating it into your daily feeling, thoughts, and life. In addition, you will understand the new reality and possibly have an insight into how you can grow forward out of grief.

Suppose you have lost someone you love or something that means a lot to you (a business, a physical ability, an idea, a relationship, or a sense of control or independence). In that case, at the acceptance stage, you understand the best decision to make is going forward. At a particular stage in life, everyone will experience bereavement and grief, but not in the same way; just as our suffering is unique, our responses will also be different. And as you journey down the road, experiencing changes in the process, your goal should be changing your life for the better.

You should not interpret acceptance as feeling happy about a loss or pretending that what happened has not or will not occur; it means you accept both the loss and the pain experienced and are ready to move on and plan for your future. It means embracing the bad and good things you feel in the present can be used to turn your life around positively. At the acceptance stage, you will start to take good care of yourself, develop a sense of self-compassion, and cope and adapt to the circumstances. Furthermore, express yourself in an assertive, honest, and open manner; feel optimistic; engage with reality precisely the way it is and not your thoughts about it; feel more relaxed and secure; be vulnerable and allow your emotions to have their way; be more present and mindful and find new meaning.

Have you been bereaved? What should your aim be, particularly if you have been battling with the pain for a long time? With acceptance, you will make peace with the crisis event and move along without sadness and pain. Besides, the good times you had with the person you lost and the great memories you cherished will come to your mind instead of despair. There were once two friends, Melissa and Amy; they were best friends in their high school days. After graduation, they were still very much together. However, some years passed, and the friends did not see each other as they usually did because of responsibilities and life changes. During this period of inconsistency, which lasted about a decade, Melissa had become an alcohol addict and was struggling with the condition; she tried her best to be free from the addiction and to be treated for the illness she was battling. Finally, after a long time, Amy saw Melissa, and there came a day both reconnected. Both friends were so glad to see each other— oh! There were lots of stories to share.

Seeing her best friend, Melissa could not help but pay Amy a long, meaningful visit. But a few days later, the unfortunate happened; Melissa was declared dead of a heart attack. What bad news for Amy! Amy grieved her friend but did not allow the grief to overwhelm her. Instead, she was grateful that fate led them to see each other again before Melissa's eternal departure. For Amy to do well at the acceptance stage, she must understand some important things; the first was that due to the addiction struggle Melissa experienced, Amy had been bracing for her death for an extended period. The second was that she could now enjoy the incredible memories of their friendship, and lastly was that their friendship was genuine to the extent that it could endure time apart from each other and addiction.

Another related story is that of Maggie, who lost a precious child to the grim reaper. On a tragic day, Ann was so filled with juvenile energy after finishing her last day of school; all she was interested in was how she would ride her bike and show her skill off to other children in the neighborhood. Maggie was inside since she was on her afternoon off but consented to Ann enjoying her bike; the unfortunate happened. Someone screamed suddenly, and Maggie could hear it from inside the house. Ann was struck by Maggie's next-door neighbor's car while on her bike. An ambulance was called, and Ann was hospitalized, but she never survived the head injury she sustained from the accident. Maggie grieved and had to live with the guilt for a long time. As she got to the acceptance stage, she could live a normal life. Maggie's experiences during the acceptance phase included brief feelings of joy and laughter; a faint vision of how she could live without Ann; and acknowledging that she would never stop grieving Ann's death, but she could still live fine.

For divorce or long-term relationship breakup, you will not be focusing on what led to the separation but on the experiences and learnings you got from the relationship. Then, you will aim at how you can have a brighter future. Let me tell you a brief story about two intimate friends, Shari and Jeff; they had been close friends since college. After graduation and securing jobs, they hardly had the time for themselves anymore, and their interest in the same things began to shift. But due to how close they once were and how long they had been together, they decided not to end the relationship. However, Jeff later thought that breaking it would be the ideal option for them; this was a tough decision for Jeff, but what they did was rational. After the breakup, Jeff struggled with loneliness and adaptation to an independent life. He later overcame his struggles and became more comfortable after months of separation; this happened because he was able to acknowledge the breakup with Shari. He understood three different things.

The first was that before the idea of a breakup was raised, he was never oblivious to the fact that both had been drifting apart; he was only scared of losing his friend. The second was that he was okay handling some things independently, though loneliness sometimes engulfed him. The third things were that he noticed he was then unable to handle some things in his life by himself without the help of Shari, but now, after living alone, he has built confidence in his life.

For being diagnosed with a terminal illness, you will not be focusing on how you can fight against the result. Instead, you will put your heart to and channel your energy toward doing things you can do that can make you impactful within the time you have left. An excellent example of this event is the case of Stephen Hawking, which we discussed in the previous chapter. Even after being told that all he had to live was just two to four years, Hawking stayed motivated and focused his energy on learning. As fate would have it, he did not only shift his own life to be better but also lived until the age of seventy-six. Rather than struggling with the diagnosis, Hawking understood that for his life to be better, he needed to focus on something that could make life worthwhile while he was still alive.

For experiencing financial loss, your focus should not be on what you have done or not done that led to such a situation but on being optimistic about life and moving on to a better future. Chad and Liz, two intimate friends, give a great example. Chad and Liz decided to open a new restaurant and bar downtown. For the first few months of business, both could not believe how great the enterprise had turned out to be. Then, unfortunately, a night came when a thunderstorm occurred; their hope of growing the business was shattered the same night as flooding rains destroyed most parts of the building. The damage was so extensive that Chad and Liz had no option but to close the business and face a financial loss reluctantly. The grief from the loss caused them intense emotional pain. But they later summoned the courage to accept the financial loss as something that had already happened, which there was nothing they could do to change. Acknowledging this fact helped them move on emotionally, as well. There were three things Chad and Liz understood that helped them. The first thing was that they still had significant, enjoyable memories of when the business was flourishing; the second was that they could now optimistically focus on a better future. The third thing was that they now had the experience of financial loss and learned the ability to survive it or find a way through.

What about missing a significant life event? In this situation, your focus shouldn't be on what you will miss; you should rather be hopeful that as long as you're still living, more opportunities are still in the future. Jessie and Julie were blood sisters with a solid bond — they saw each other as confidants and would always do what they could to make each other happy. For months, Jessie left home to work in Germany, leaving her sister in the United States. But she now had to return home to see Julie, who would be going for a long-term overseas military deployment. "I need to see my sister before she leaves," Jessie said anxiously. Unfortunately, the day Jessie planned to return to the United States, airline security developed an unexpected issue, leading to the cancellation of thousands of flights, including hers. Stranded in Germany, Jessie did not know what she could do since she could not fly for the next fourteen days. Due to this, Jessie was unable to see her sister before she departed. Like anyone would do for a loved one, Jessie grieved for losing such a chance; she even thought such a loss would not have occurred if she had left Germany earlier. Jessie struggled with this feeling of guilt for some time, but she later accepted the situation by considering three things. She first acknowledged that she could have done nothing to avoid the missed flight. The second thing she accepted was that she was sad not to have seen her sister before leaving — and missing her departure was unexpected — but it probably would not be the last time she would see her. The third thing she acknowledged was that there were other ways both could stay connected throughout Julie's deployment.

It would help if you remembered that before the acceptance stage is the depression phase. So, before accepting the new reality, you will most likely be overwhelmed by sadness, lethargy, brain fog, and physical pain. Notwithstanding, since grief stages are rarely orderly, the next stage may not be accepted. You may return to the anger stage, or any other stage, before moving back to the acceptance stage for the new reality adjustment.

The acceptance stage is a stage you would like to remain in, but emotions may sometimes be unpredictable; there is a tendency that you will see yourself coping differently each day. That is, a day will come when you feel great, while another day will show up when you feel more challenged. With this, you may still experience loneliness, anxiety, and fear, though you have acknowledged your loss.

So, you should not feel bad or begin to judge yourself unfairly — you should see it as a normal grief process. As you live your day-to-day life, your emotions will continue to stabilize. In addition, dedicated events in your life can trigger feelings of grief, including family events, holidays, and anniversaries. As a lucky person to have reached the acceptance stage, you will be able to accept your loss, notice the changed situations, and shift your life for the better.

Your memories are a crucial part of your existence; as you find them easier to embrace, you can also find them less stressful to discuss. I will even advise you to focus on celebrating those you have lost instead of sitting in the corner of your room feeling mournful about how you have missed them.

Acceptance and Misconceptions

People have different perceptions about the acceptance stage of grief; one of these is how it is seen as a "carrot at the end of the stick." From their understanding, they show that if you can do a specific thing, you can get a particular outcome. This claim can be true on the surface, but on the deeper ground, the notion of acceptance is beyond that; it is a grief stage with a different system of accomplishment compared to other tasks you may set out to handle. Let us go through some common misconceptions people have about acceptance.

Acceptance is an essential part of life. It is the ability to accept and embrace who we are, our circumstances, and the people around us. It is the ability to be comfortable with ourselves and our environment and to be open to change. Unfortunately, many misconceptions about acceptance can lead to misunderstanding and even conflict.

One of the most common misconceptions about acceptance is that it means giving up. This is not true. Acceptance does not mean giving up on goals or dreams; instead, it is the ability to accept the current situation and move forward with life. Another misconception about acceptance is that it means being weak or passive. This is also not true. Acceptance is a sign of strength and resilience. It is the ability to recognize limitations and to work within them. It is the ability to accept circumstances and to make the best of them. A third misconception about acceptance is that it means not taking into consideration bad behavior. Rather, it is the ability to recognize our limitations and work within them. Finally, a fourth misconception about acceptance is giving up our power. It is not necessarily truthful, for it signifies strength and resilience. It is essential to recognize the misconceptions about acceptance and to understand that it is not about giving up, being weak, condoning bad behavior, or giving up our power.

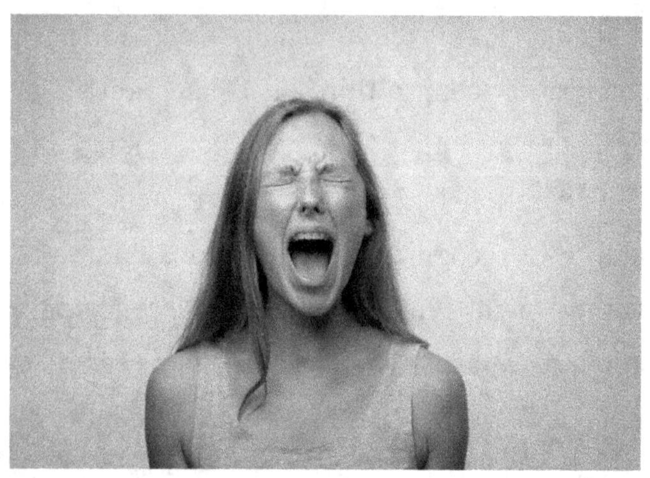

Misconception #1: Constancy

Grief is an emotion that is often difficult to cope with and understand. It can be a very isolating experience, and it can be hard to know how to move forward. One way to cope with grief is to focus on constancy. Constancy in grief can find a sense of stability and comfort during grief. It is important to remember that grief is a process, and it is not something that can be rushed or forced. As you already know, grief has various stages.

Unfortunately, several people need to be aware that each stage is a constant. I must let you know; this is untrue: the stages can overlap, run into each other, and occur without regard for order. As a griever, moving from one step to another does not mean you are through with the one you left behind. The fact is that you can still find yourself there, even after years have passed. Nevertheless, your grief challenges and the time you spend battling with it will determine how easy you will find it when revisiting a stage. The summation is that you find grief more manageable because it is a process that operates on a twisted and non-linear timeline.

Constancy in grief can help to find a sense of peace and acceptance amid grief. Constancy in grief can be found in many different ways. One way is to focus on the things that remain constant in life. This could include relationships with family and friends, faith, or hobbies and interests. Focusing on these things can provide a sense of stability and comfort in grief. It can also be helpful to find a routine that can stick. This could include going for a walk each day or taking time to meditate, or journaling. Having a routine can provide a sense of structure.

Another way to find constancy in grief is to focus on self-care. Taking time to do things that make you feel good can provide comfort and stability. This could include taking a hot bath, going for a massage, or spending time in nature. In addition, taking time to focus on yourself can provide a sense of peace and acceptance.

Finally, it can be helpful to find a support system. This could include family, friends, or a support group. Having people to talk to and lean on can provide comfort, and talking to a therapist or counselor can provide guidance and support.

Misconception #2: Normalcy

You will see how some individuals explain acceptance as a grief stage when everything you face returns to normal. Can this be true? Let us take, for instance, if you lose a loved one that holds a significant part of your support system — will this loss not affect every aspect of your life? Yes, it will. And as a matter of fact, there is no way you can bring the dead back. So, going back to the previous normal is not possible. However, you can move forward with your life to build a new one that appears comfortable, just like the old one you had lived before. It is important to face reality; healing from grief undoubtedly takes time, and every griever has a specific amount of time.

Normalcy is a concept that is often taken for granted, but it is an essential part of life which conforms to the accepted standards of behavior and appearance. It is a way of life that is comfortable and familiar, and it is something to strive for. It gives a sense of belonging, security, and acceptance, which helps to feel like you are part of something larger than yourself. Normalcy is also vital because it helps us to maintain mental and physical health. When in a state of normalcy, it is more likely to be able to cope with stress and anxiety and more likely to be able to maintain a healthy lifestyle. Normalcy also helps us feel more connected and safe to the environment, and it helps us feel more connected to the people around us, like a part of a larger community.

Therefore, nothing says acceptance means returning to normal; it is only a stage where you develop a new coping ability to deal with life as it comes without those you love.

Misconception #3: No More Grieving

Some people believe that grief is a lifetime process, while others think that after some significant amount of time spent grieving, their life can go back to normal, feeling no grief over their loss. Note that the acceptance stage is not the stoppage point for grief; it is never the end of it. The stage is only a level where you get a more peaceful continuation of your loss. The only thing is the peace and comfort you will enjoy that you cannot find in the other phases. I advise you to be different from some grievers that focus on unrealistic improvement with no regard for comprehension of the non-linear dimension of the bereavement stages.

No more grieving after a loss is an impossible dream; it is a necessary part of the healing process. It is a way of expressing sadness and pain and honoring the person or thing they have lost. Grief is a complex emotion that can take many forms and last for a long time. It is a way of acknowledging the loss and allowing ourselves to feel the pain and sadness that comes with it. Having to express in many different ways, such as through tears, talking about the loss, writing about it, or engaging in activities that help remember the person or thing lost. It can be a time to reflect, grow and heal as part of the learning experience. It can also be a time to connect with others who have experienced similar losses and to find comfort and support in each other. No one can tell you how long grief will last or how you should grieve. Everyone grieves differently, and finding what works best for you is crucial. It is not something to be ashamed of or to try to avoid. It is a part of life and something to go through to heal and move forward to find purpose in life after a loss.

Signals When Reaching Acceptance

One of the shared questions people ask is how to recognize the moments that will tell them if they are heading toward acceptance. The exciting part of this is that there are numerous ways to know that the progress of your emotional state is achieved while you're struggling with grief.

Reaching acceptance is a process that can be both rewarding and challenging. It is a journey of self-discovery and growth that can take time and effort to achieve. Moving through this process, specific signals can indicate that acceptance has been reached.

One of the most common signals of reaching acceptance is a feeling of peace and contentment. When you have accepted a situation or circumstance, you often feel a sense of calm and inner peace, which can signify that you have come to terms with the situation and are no longer struggling against it. Another signal of reaching acceptance is a feeling of clarity. When accepting a situation, one gains a new perspective on it and can see the situation more objectively and understand it better. This can lead to clarity and understanding that can signify acceptance. A third signal of reaching acceptance is a feeling of empowerment. When you accept a situation, you feel more in control, more confident and capable of making decisions and taking action. This can be a sign that you have accepted the situation and are ready to move forward. Finally, a fourth signal of reaching acceptance is a feeling of gratitude. When you have accepted a situation and feel grateful for the experience, thus being thankful for the lessons learned and the growth and experiences, this can signify that you have accepted the situation and are ready to move on. Recognizing the signals of approval and gaining insight are positive indications of acceptance.

Dissipation of the Thoughts of Your Loss

It is normal to dwell on the thought of those you have lost when you start to grieve; these thoughts can even overwhelm you. From time to time, you would contemplate what led to such an event — it could even become difficult for you to stop the thought from coming back to you or resist it once it takes hold. Reaching acceptance is gradual. You can notice a small amount of acceptance early in the grief process. But as you move on, you will see that some positive thoughts become persistent; these positive thoughts may include those you have about the legacy of your loved one, your future, and the workings of death and life.

Focus on the positive aspects of life. It is important to remember the good times shared with the person who passed away and to focus on the memories that bring joy. It is also essential to focus on what you can still do and find ways to enjoy life. Finally, finding healthy ways to cope with the pain is important, as this can help lessen the intensity of the thoughts of loss. With time and effort, the thoughts of loss will eventually dissipate. As a result, you will begin to feel extreme sorrow, rage, and denial less often. The moment you start to see these signals, then you are moving toward acceptance.

Embracing the Thoughts About Your Loss

For me to tell you not to avoid thinking about your loss may sound contradictory to the first point, but it is not. Yes, it is acceptable that you are not dwelling on those you have lost, which means you are on your way to the acceptance stage. Nevertheless, it does not imply that you will not think about such an individual. On the contrary, doing such may impede your healing in the long run. At one point, you might hear people say it's not advisable to bottle up negative emotions; grief comes with intense and unpredictable emotions at the early stage. At this point, you might find it helpful to avoid grief expressions. However, it is a method that could have a negative effect. And this could be hindering your ability to deal with your loss head-on in a healthy way. On the surface, you may see people who practice bottling up their emotions appear to be strong when it comes to overseeing their feelings; but the story may change if, by any chance, someone brings up their loved one. You will find it sustainable if you can talk about your crisis event regularly, preferably with a trusted confidant, regardless of how painful your situation can be. Doing this continuously will help you to be in control of your grief rather than your grief controlling you.

One way to embrace the thoughts about loss is to talk about it. Talking about loss can help to process emotions and can help to feel less alone. Write about a loss in a journal or blog. Another way to embrace the thoughts about loss is to find ways to honor the person or thing you lost by creating a memorial or a tribute to them. Find ways to keep their memories alive by telling stories about them or creating a photo album. It is also vital to take care of yourself during this time, find activities that bring joy, and help cope with loss.

Finally, it is essential to remember that it is okay not to be okay. It is okay to feel sad, angry or overwhelmed. Being gentle with yourself and giving time to heal is important.

Avoiding Resenting Your Loss

A good signal to pay attention to when approaching the acceptance phase is that you can think about those you have lost without resenting their death. Of course, you already know how emotionally unhelpful and unhealthy it can be to bottle up your feelings, so it is never a bad idea to think and speak about your loss. Grief is a natural response to loss, and it is important to recognize these feelings and process them in a healthy way. Bu t it is crucial that while thinking about someone you lost, you avoid lamenting that you will not see them again. If you can do this, it shows that you are ready to accept the loss and prepare to shift to become a better person.

So let me tell you this: you are on the right path to recovery from loss if moments with your loved one can come to mind without looking at it from the angle of the eventual bereavement.

Approving Memorialization

One of the significant symptoms of grief is to disapprove of the actions of doctors, funeral directors, end-of-life care providers, and family members in doing their death-related duties. It is expected that when you lose someone you love, you should be reclusive and sorrowful. But that is not all: other typical behaviors you will show when you lose someone you love include being defensive, critical, angry, and generally difficult to deal with. Your reaction could also include detesting everything surrounding a death. Nevertheless, the moment all these signs start to wane, it could be said to be a positive indication that you are approaching a higher stage of grief. At this mature stage, you are memorializing your loved one will be something with which you are satisfied.

Approving memorialization is a necessary process that helps to ensure that the memory of a person who has passed away is honored and respected in a way that is appropriate and meaningful.

Self-Support Systems Through Acceptance

When working your way through the acceptance phase of grief, there are different supports you can provide for yourself. Self-care is wonderful; no one can know you more than you know yourself. With self-care strategies, you can easily take your power back in grief and show up in a better way.

This concept encourages individuals to accept circumstances to better cope with life's challenges and better manage emotions and reactions to difficult situations. This can lead to improved mental health, self-confidence, and relationships.

One way to practice acceptance is to focus on the things that can be controlled. This can include thoughts, feelings, and behaviors. Also, focus on what to improve current circumstances. This can include setting goals, developing new skills, and seeking help. It is about recognizing our current reality and finding ways to cope, which can help to manage emotions and reactions to difficult situations.

Accept Your Emotional Process

Having mixed feelings when grieving is not unusual, but you must learn how to accept them. As easy as it may sound, it never is when it comes to reality; this is because it will appear like giving up on who or what you have lost. And this is when you begin to feel unmatched emotions such as emptiness, sadness, and peacefulness. Accepting your loss does not mean you are completely okay with your loss — there are times at this stage you will question your perception; this is never strange during the acceptance phase.

Recognize and accept emotions, even if they are uncomfortable or difficult to process. It helps to understand reactions better and recognize feelings in different situations. As a result, learn to manage emotions and use them to your advantage. Remember that emotions are valid and essential. Identify what triggers different emotions and how to react to them. Understand how to empathize with the feelings of others and learn to be more compassionate towards their emotional process.

So, you must learn how to manage your emotions, even if they are painful. It is a wonderful way to care for yourself. And since there are no wrong emotions when it comes to grieving, you must acknowledge and accept your emotional process.

Talk to Someone About Your Improvement

You should find someone to talk to about your movement toward the acceptance stage. Here, you will tell such an individual about your feelings and thoughts. With this, both your feelings and thoughts will be made less intense. It is normal for you to see it as challenging at first to pour out how you are feeling during this time using words, and even the fear of uttering something with certainty may overwhelm you. But when you summon the courage to say what is on your mind, it will help strengthen your reality. Although it may appear that you will be hurt in this way, the truth is it will not hurt you but will shift you toward feeling better than before.

Talking to someone about it can be a great way to get started when looking to improve life. Talking to someone can help clarify what to achieve and how to achieve it. It can also give an outside perspective and be accountable. When talking to someone about your improvement, be honest, and open about goals and progress. It is important to remember that improvement takes time and effort; stay motivated and focused. Explain what you want to achieve and why it is essential to you. Share successes and challenges and ask for advice and feedback to help stay on track. It is also essential to be realistic about what to accomplish and how long it will take. When choosing someone to talk to, it is crucial to find someone who is supportive and understanding. This could be a friend, family member, mentor, or professional. Finding someone knowledgeable and experienced in the area you are looking to improve is also important. Be bold and ask questions and be willing to take advice. Everyone has different experiences and perspectives, and it is crucial to respect that.

The bottom line is that you will feel more at peace after talking about someone you lost. But when you decide to express what's in your heart to someone you see as a confidant, it will help you avoid isolation, get needed support, and help you cope with the situation much more confidently.

Get Enough Rest

Processing is nothing but emotional work. Yes, acceptance is a stage where you feel emotional ease and inner peace, but it does not mean there are no ups and downs at this stage. A true acceptance of loss is characterized by letting go of the reality that you have been accommodating in your existence for a long time; you will find this action painful, though you understand perfectly that it is time.

You may get distracted and agitated by your emotions and may even experience mixed feelings of doubt and peace. No one will go through that and not feel exhausted because attempting to cope with the waves of emotions can cost you the mental energy needed for other things. After making various adjustments, it will become inexorable for you not to feel physically and mentally sapped before the end of the day. This is why I advise you to handle your plan and schedule easily in case you experience more downtime than expected. With this, you will be able to feel re-energized after some time. In some days and weeks, however, you may need to get plenty of rest to get through.

Support From Others Through Acceptance

Sometimes, you may not be able to deal with your challenges by yourself; this is usually when you do not feel ready to accept that you have lost someone. As a solid emotional phase, you may need to find the proper support and tools that can help you process the layered and complex emotions to avoid getting trapped in your pain. It would be fantastic if you could get your family and friends to help you embrace your new reality.

Support from others through acceptance is a significant part of life. It is essential for mental and emotional well-being, and it is the difference between feeling secure and feeling isolated. Acceptance from others can come in many forms, from a simple smile or kind word to a hug or a listening ear which can help us to feel more connected to people. You can be more open to talking about struggles, seeking help, and giving and receiving support, which can help build strong and lasting relationships. It is a sign of respect, understanding, and appreciation. When accepted by others, it can help to feel confident and comfortable in your skin, which can help to manage emotions and stress better. It feels more open to trying new things and taking risks to know that a support system is in place.

Knowing What You Have Already Accepted

Are you feeling the total emotional weight of your loss while you are already in the acceptance stage? It does not matter if you are prepared for this process. It may still appear overwhelming for some time; your thoughts will center around the harsh reality, and you wonder how you can move along. This is where others can come in for support by reminding you of the difficult things you have overcome in the past — they can help you understand that, though the pain may be too intense, it won't feel like that forever. Besides, they will make you realize that you are moving forward is possible, even if you are pessimistic at the moment. And they will show you that a part of you is aware of the power of resilience, even if you may feel broken.

Awareness of the beliefs and values you have already accepted is crucial to making informed decisions, identifying areas of your life that may need to be changed or improved, and moving along in life. This can help you grow and develop as a person and to become more open-minded. In addition, consider being mindful of decisions that may affect others to make decisions that are more considerate and respectful of others which can open to new ideas and perspectives.

Providing Support When You Are Emotional and Uncertain

As you move on, learning to accept your loss, you may experience periods of uncertainty. At first, you may struggle with this, but later, you can move past it. Nonetheless, you should note that after moving past your uncertainty, there is a high tendency that you may become deeply emotional. When you accept a significant loss, you automatically embrace the pain that comes with it; when you try to express this feeling and pain, it can come with an overwhelming impact. Others will be there to help you when you finally decide to release the force of your feelings that you have been holding for a long time. Their support will come warmly, telling you that it is okay and that the pain you feel is an essential part of the acceptance process.

It is helpful to have someone to provide emotional support and understanding, process emotions and gain clarity on the situation, and provide reassurance and encouragement. It reduces feelings of isolation and loneliness. Knowing that someone is there to talk to and who is there to listen can be a great source of comfort, especially during times of uncertainty, providing a sense of hope. The fact that you have someone to turn to can help to provide the optimism and help motivate you to keep going. It is incredibly beneficial and makes all the difference during difficult times.

Acknowledging Your Pain in Your Unique Process

Indeed, everyone will not grieve the same way. And this is where others come in to support you in your unique journey rather than imposing their personal grief experience on yours; others should come with no intention of making it about themselves. They would understand that when they talk about their loss, even if it may appear helpful, it can make them feel like their personal experience is being overshadowed or dismissed; it may also sound like they are forcing how they think you should grieve on to you.

There is nothing wrong with asking them how they cope with grief and listening to how they share their experiences and what they think may help you with your situation, but the knowledge they share must be channeled in more neutral ways. They, too, had traveled down the same road and faced the difficulty of the journey. So, they will not be wasting your time boring you with details about themselves but will help you accept your pain and support you as you explore your unique process.

Acknowledging the pain allows you to take ownership of it and begin understanding it. It is essential to recognize that pain is unique to you and that it cannot be compared to anyone else's. Acknowledging pain can help to identify its source of it and to begin to work through it. Moreover, it is okay to feel pain and to express it healthily. Acknowledging the pain creates a plan for healing to help recognize the areas of life that need to be addressed to create a more positive and fulfilling life. Finally, find the strength and courage to continue on a journey of healing and growth.

Chapter Six

Empowerment

Lea Michele Sarfati is an American singer, songwriter, actor, and author. When speaking about her late boyfriend, Cory Monteith, she talked about how grief as a process comes with empowerment.

Lea says on *The Ellen DeGeneres Show* that one of the things people are yet to understand is that, compared to staying at home, staying in the house, and checking a closet to see a pair of shoes, going to work is not in any way harder. She shows that the moment life happens to you and you become a victim of grief, it becomes part of you –and you will have no option but to live with it every day of your life, irrespective of whatever you do. You will continue to grieve when the moments are wrong and when they are great. So, she submits that rather than staying at home. She would prefer to be at work with those she loves and find comfort in knowing they are going through a similar issue.

Moreover, Lea emphasizes the words of her mother, who went through numerous losses in life. She says her mother told her that empowerment comes with grief; it is inevitable that it would be found at some point and with incredible difficulty.

Also, a time will come when the opportunity will be available to decide either to fall from it or to rise through it. As for the loss of her boyfriend, Lea says she has decided to do her best for him because she knows perfectly well that he would have done the same for her.

As someone that has experienced the death of a loved one, I can tell you that the impact it can have on your life is significant. Several individuals say this impact is a loss of control, but I can say it is a big rip-off. As a griever, a time will come when you suddenly feel that you are no longer in control of yourself.

You will find it challenging to organize your thoughts, your emotional energy will become almost nonexistent, and your emotions will be something else; you did not plan to be bereaved. Death comes visiting and leaves grief behind, leaving you with no option but to decide what to do next with your life. Since it is an unplanned occurrence, you now need to struggle with the details you have no intention of thinking about, let alone accepting. You will constantly feel devastated, helpless, and lonely during this stage.

These emotional crises will strongly push you to desire some control in your life. You know it has been a long since you felt in control, and now you are ready to take your power back: this is empowerment. Life has happened already by taking someone close to you, and you have realized that there is nothing you can do to change the past. First, you could feel the shock, and the world appeared to be moving slowly.

Then you push yourself to process it, but the emotions that have now taken over are causing confusion, bringing tears to your face, and yelling. Your desire will go back in time before the crisis event because you find it hard to endure the intense emotional pain that has come upon you. But, since this is impossible, you will pull yourself together and allow yourself to break down when it is expected. Then, you will do all you can to make each day great and let the things of the past be in the past; you will still experience the infrequent visitation of sorrow in your present. This is when you understand that the end has not come; you still have the chance to start fresh again. Meanwhile, the only way to get to this spot is to give yourself the needed support at the onset of your grieving process.

Empowerment is an inner strength born out of choice; it is both a process and a quest toward gaining more power and confidence.

To be empowered means that you are ready to advocate for yourself by recognizing how important it is for you to change and equipping yourself with the strength to take the appropriate steps toward achieving the desired outcome.

Through empowerment, you will give yourself the necessary education about grief. You will not be ignorant of what could trigger your negative emotions, how to feel the feelings, the related benefits, and when to say "no."

Precisely, empowerment is a process of learning about yourself.

Empowerment can also be seen as a process of creating boundaries; this is essential when grieving. Setting these boundaries will help you limit the invasion of negative thoughts, people, and objects - it is crucial that you understand yourself and how you can live in your grief. In addition, doing this will help you recognize your comfort zone and where your safety is; everyone has the choice of staying within their boundaries.

In addition, empowerment can be a process of pursuing your goals daily. You can break down your goals and strive to accomplish a feasible number on a daily basis; this can be one, two, or three things you know you can do successfully per day. Besides, it does not matter if the goals are small or big – what should be your concern is if they can be attained.

It would be challenging to experience an ideal quality of life when you are overwhelmed with grief or going through the impacts of loss caused by divorce, death, or lifestyle changes. This is when you will find yourself drowning in the pool of unhappiness or find it arduous to break the chain of the constant ache of heartbreak. During this time, you may feel lonely, isolated, and incomplete, but since you have made up your mind to break free from the bondage that grief has placed you, empowerment allows you to see positive changes. I will tell you that it can be scary to go on with such a decision; nevertheless, you cannot see any changes if you do not try. Eric Clapton shows that when you are trying to heal yourself of your pain, your goal is not to make it go away entirely but to make it part of who you are after the loss.

Empowerment: An Effective Way to Mobilize Strength for Change

Are you suffering from the emotional pain you get through grief? Empowerment is a process that serves as a means of escapism. You can find your capacities and strengths to control your life with them. The term "empowerment" is defined in counseling as the belief that those dealing with a loss can take care of their own lives through proper management.

As far as empowerment is concerned, one of the components you stand to get is self-determination; through this, you recognize your choices and become encouraged to make independent decisions. This implies that no one will have to do for you that you can do for yourself.

Your case may be that you are from a marginalized or disadvantaged group, where you have been thoroughly dealt with by abuse, poverty, oppression, or any adverse life experiences; you really need to get a better life for your family and yourself.

Empowerment is an effective way to mobilize strength for change and gain control because it encourages you to take ownership of your life and become an active change agent. It is a process of recognizing and utilizing the strengths to create a collective power this encourages thinking critically and making decisions that are in the best interests. This encourages thinking outside the box and coming up with innovative solutions to problems to take risks and be creative. Finally, empowerment is an effective way to mobilize strength for change and to create a more equitable and just society.

Nonetheless, your powerlessness can keep pulling you down the ladder of making the necessary changes, instilling in you a pervasive sense of failure, and feeling rejected by or different from others. I want you to know that this lack of power in you can be because of your low self-esteem and negative self-evaluation or your lack of confidence in your strength and capacity to improve your life. But the loss you have experienced is powerful enough to give you the hope you need to move along to a brighter future that exists on the horizon.

How You Can Find Empowerment for Yourself

Not all experiences are universal, but one of the universal ones you can feel as a being of emotion is grief. No matter how you choose to cope with your loss, the sure thing is that how you reflect on your loss can offer valuable lessons that can guide you for your lifetime. In the preliminary stages of grief, this may look impossible, but when you find empowerment in times of crisis, it can be a valuable tool for healing. I have never denied that grief may be one of the most harrowing experiences you will have in your life, but this same process can help you find strength. So, how can you find empowerment for yourself?

Empowerment has the confidence to make decisions that are best for you. It is a process of self-discovery and self-actualization that becomes the best version of yourself with goals with action. Taking action is the only way to make progress toward achieving goals. It is also essential to be patient and persistent. Do not give up; if there are no results right away, keep taking action, and eventually, you will see progress. Finally, make time for yourself and do things that make you feel good. This could include exercising, meditating, reading, or spending time with friends and family. Taking care of yourself and concentrating on being motivated on the journey to finding empowerment would define your purpose and happiness.

Identifying Your Skills, Strength, and Passions

Instead of focusing on how helpless and powerless you have become, you can channel the energy to analyzing the number of times you have felt empowered and had the strength to take action. You can efficiently deal with helplessness and powerlessness and find empowerment by becoming aware of the situations and emotions you had around these scenarios. For example, you may want to consider how you felt in your body when you felt empowered, the thoughts that came to your mind, the actions you took, the supports you had, and what worked well for you – all these can give you what you need to take charge of your current situation.

Moreover, apart from seeking emotional support by talking to others about your experiences, you may also want to look into yourself to find motivations and reasons you must move along. Since you have goals, you are looking forward to achieving, you can tap into them by reminding yourself how important it is to actualize them. Besides, you will need to constantly tell yourself how crucial you need to attain your life's purpose and to live up to your highest core values.

Sometimes when life happens, it can affect several things about you, like changing your life's purpose and shifting your values; you may want to see this as usual and accept the changes. But you must focus on how you can move your life forward and hold onto your past.

Identifying skills, strengths, and passions is integral to self-discovery, personal growth, and development. Understanding your potential could make decisions that align with your values and goals. Skills are the abilities that you have acquired through experience, education, or training. They can include technical skills, such as coding or accounting, and soft skills, such as communication or problem-solving. In addition, they can include qualities such as resilience, creativity, or leadership. Finally, identifying strengths can help to understand what makes you stand out and how you can use those qualities and interests to reach goals, thus getting through a present circumstance.

Here, you may want to consider the most crucial thing in your life: your new life's vision and purpose for the one you had changed, how you can work toward your future, your core values, and how you can start living these core values daily. You must take things gradually, one step at a time. If you are now setting your course toward a new direction, then your movement must not be too early or too quick; you must be strategic and plan purposefully. Besides, there are other things you need to look for as you move along the new path – these include gaining comfort in human contact, finding solace when self-reflecting and relaxing, and gaining comfort in small pleasures. You should also take care of yourself – particularly your body – and ensure that your foundations are solid for your decision to move forward.

Learning to Share with and Support One Another

Although your crisis event may be different from others, there is a higher possibility that you will feel a great deal of pain when you experience loss and grief. Sometimes, we go to those around us for help and support when we are facing some emotional challenges in our lives. Notwithstanding, you will not be the only person feeling the pain of loss when someone dies due to how grieving is a shared experience. At the beginning of the grief, especially before or during the funeral, everyone's emotions will be high, and they will begin to deal with the grief personally.

Even though it may be difficult to help one another during this period, you can tap into why the deceased was essential to you and develop a sense of compassion for those around you, helping them find peace and strength. Besides, the period of shared grieving can be an opportunity for you to strengthen your relationships with others by learning how to communicate with and support them.

There is something else you must know: grief will not just offer you lessons about being compassionate toward others. It will also educate you on how you can do the same for yourself in order for you to feel empowered and at peace. Well, it is normal for you to see grieving as being more difficult if you are charged with organizing a funeral in the family or have other related duties on your shoulders. But rather than dealing with these feelings intrinsically, why not give yourself moments of grief to put the responsibilities in perspective? Then, while grieving, you will learn how valuable and fragile life is and get encouraged to have compassion on yourself and be at peace with your feelings. This is an excellent asset as you move along in the affairs of your life.

Support is essential for building strong relationships, creating a sense of community, and fostering a healthy environment for a safe and supportive group where everyone feels valued in many ways, from simply listening to a friend's problems to helping with a project. It can build a bond that can last a lifetime, thus making you feel connected and building trust. Support from time to time can be a great way to show someone that you care, like helping out with a project or just being there for someone. It would create resilience and help to cope with difficult situations.

Practicing Creative Visualization

Christy Monson, MFT, an author and retired psychotherapist, said that what forms our feelings is our thinking; so, there is a need to change our thinking first to change our feelings. By creative visualization, I am referring to when you daydream with a purpose; it has been proven to be an effective practice to heal you emotionally, create a sense of calm, and connect you to the wisdom within you.

According to Monson, there are steps you can take to make visualization work by connecting to your "inner child." The first step is sitting comfortably and quietly. Then, focus on your feet, your hands, and the object you are sitting on, and ask yourself to describe the light around you. The second step is inhaling and exhaling slowly via your nasal cavity, counting it. Then, close your eyes and begin to imagine a flight of stairs. See yourself ascending the stairs and counting numbers until you get to ten. Then, put the details of the stairs in mind, noticing their appearance and the feel of climbing. The sixth step is to see yourself getting to a lovely place, like a beach or mountain top, when you reach the end point of the stairs. Next, decorate the scene with anything you prefer, and use your senses to imagine how it smells, sounds, and feels.

Then, feel the healing of the child in this place. The eighth step is to care for yourself after caring for your inner child before moving to the ninth step, which is to search for another version of you in this place (a wise mentor); they can answer your questions and listen as you discuss your concerns. The tenth and ultimate step is to descend the stairs once you are done. Then, for a few minutes, try to be grateful for the person you are and the lovely place you have visited.

This above exercise can help deal with the symptoms of anxiety and depression, such as feeling helpless. Hence, you can empower yourself and take control of your life.

Creative visualization is a powerful tool that can be used to manifest dreams and goals. It is a form of mental imagery that creates a vivid picture of the goal by visualizing desired outcomes that would create powerful and positive energy to help manifest goals. The first step in practicing creative visualization is clarifying what to achieve. Take some time to think about what to manifest in your life. Then, with a clear vision,   create a mental image of it. Next, visualize yourself achieving your goal and imagine how it will feel to have it. The next step is to focus on the positive aspects of the purpose and on the positive emotions that come with it. Imagine how it will feel to have achieved the goal and how it will make life better. Once you have a clear mental image of the purpose and creative visualization to manifest it, spend some time each day visualizing the goal. Finally, take action to make the goal a reality. Take small daily steps to move closer to the goal, and use creative visualization to help you stay focused and motivated.

Living Your Life to the Fullest

There are several things a loss – particularly the death of a loved one – can make you do; it can put things in perspective and make you re-evaluate your priorities. Life is meant to be enjoyed, and everyone is entitled to live their lives to the fullest. However, this is not the case in the present age. From research, several people are seen to be living stressful, hectic, and busy lifestyles that rob most of the time they ought to use for self-reflection. Even though it may appear complex and scary to change these lifestyles, death has a way of changing things.

When you lose someone close to you, the occurrence can serve as a harsh reminder for you to know the time you have used already living and the time you have left to make yourself a better person is out of your control.

This unexpected and sudden loss often comes as a more painful and jarring awakening. Let us take, for instance: you lose a loved one to a terminal illness. In this situation, you can become encouraged to break those unhealthy habits that can lead to similar conditions. Likewise, if you see your loved one live an extraordinary life until they pass on, you can become inspired by such an experience to do the same.

Living life to the fullest is a great way to make the most of the time here on earth. Firstly, taking risks, pushing yourself out of your comfort zone, and embracing the unknown. Secondly, taking the time to appreciate the little things and making the most of every moment. Thirdly, living with intention and purpose and striving to impact the world positively. The ultimate step to living life to the fullest is to take the time and reflect. What are your goals and dreams? What do you want to accomplish? What kind of legacy to leave behind? Taking the time to think about these questions can help create a plan for how to live life. Once these are in place, it is time to start taking action. It is time to set goals and take steps to achieve them while trying new things. Taking the time to give back and help those in need is a humble act, and it is worth it. Living life to the fullest can be challenging. However, try to appreciate the little things, make the most of every moment, and live a meaningful and fulfilling life.

The point is that regardless of the reason, you may begin to feel that life is fleeting after losing a loved one; this is normal and fine, and for you to acknowledge the value in it is excellent. However, it would help if you focused on not allowing such a feeling of how transient life is to result in destructive behavior. But, if it results in a healthier and happier future, you should embrace it.

Focusing on the Future to Come

One of the things that grief can help you with is to help you focus on your future and look at it in several ways. Grief can be a complex process in its initial stages; during these phases, you may see moving on as impossible or feel like you are dishonoring or disrespecting the memory of your loved one. Even though this can be painful, grief can remind you that you can still live your life even after losing someone you love. The fact is that when you continue living after the loss in a way that the deceased would admire, then you can have memories and experiences for the coming generations.

The hardest part of grieving is remembering the past while working toward creating a better future for yourself. In this process, you may fail on either side of the spectrum; some individuals believe that the ideal way to oversee their situation is to put away everything that can trigger the memories of those they have lost. In contrast, others may believe that the best way they can oversee the situation is to fill their residence with sentimental items and photographs of those they have lost, so they can be reminded of the great times they spent with them.

This is to show that people do not grieve the same way. And in fact, there is no standard method to deal with grief or any part of the process. If you are in a terrible situation of being affected by the memories of someone, you have lost. You can try to focus only on the happy and positive things you can remember about them while you never stop living your own life. With this, you will be astonished at how much progress you will make in shifting your life to become a better person.

Furthermore, you can become empowered and encouraged by accessing your memories of how your loved one lived; this can be an opportunity for you to learn from what they lived through, including their experiences, mistakes, and achievements. The lessons you get from the dead can constantly remind you that they now exist in your memory, positively influencing your choices.

It is crucial to have a vision for the future and to strive to make it a reality. Be mindful of the present and ensure that steps are directed to a bright and full of possibilities for the future. With the past and experiences learned, you can make better decisions. Invest in yourself and the potential of the future by learning new skills, taking classes, and in education.

Developing a Sense of Gratitude

Have you ever been approached by someone while grieving and been told it is better to have and lost than not to have had it at all? As precise as this statement may look and as nearly illogical as it may sound, it can help when dealing with losing someone you love. "To have" can be seen as a burden you do not need because you have it; that is why you will need to endure the pain when you eventually lose it. Nonetheless, many people are so grateful for the moments they spend with their loved ones; they see it as a special gift from fate. Even though death is not something anyone would wish for, it is still a gift all the same; but being grateful is one of the best and most potent tools for you while grieving because of the loss.

If you check, several people live in this world without familial bonds or someone dear or close to them. For those that do, when you lose such as individual, you will find the grieving process much harder. Nevertheless, it will remind you that you are lucky to have people in your life for whom you wish you would still live. You may not even think of this when you start grieving; it may take some time, another loss, and practice before you arrive at it. When you finally do, your feeling of grief can change from a negative experience to a hopeful or positive one, which is a given opportunity for you to cherish the connection between you and your loved one.

Gratitude can help in appreciating the good things in life and be thankful for the people and experiences that have made you who you are. Gratitude can also help to be more mindful in actions and generous with time and resources. Practice mindfulness is being aware of the present moment and being open to the experiences that come with it. Using gratitude journaling is the practice of writing down things you are thankful for. Appreciate people and experiences that have shaped you and be more thankful for them.

Preparing for Grief Triggers

It would help if you prepared yourself for several moments in the future that can trigger grief when you find yourself in a more positive mood. Some of the common grief triggers include anniversaries, birthdays, and holidays; these can string up old emotional experiences and painful memories of the past. But preparing yourself for any of these moments will empower you against the effects they may have on your emotions later.

Let us take, for instance, that you may find it challenging to handle staying alone these days, so you plan to spend the days with your family or friends. An alternative strategy is to get a spiritual book you can read when you feel overwhelmed by your emotions. Next, you must choose the management system that works for you. But before this, you need to start by recognizing what these things are. Then, you can proceed to deal with the effect they may have on your emotions.

Grief triggers can be challenging to manage, but there are some steps to take to prepare for them. The first step is recognizing that grief triggers are a normal part of the grieving process. It is essential to understand that grief triggers can be unpredictable and come from various sources. It is also important to remember that grief triggers can be positive and negative. The next step is to identify your triggers. This can be done by reflecting on past experiences and noting situations or events that can intensify grief. Finally, understand your triggers and how to manage them. Engaging in a calming activity such as yoga or meditation to cope with grief triggers could lessen the impact on emotions.

Avoiding Addictions

One of the things that can stop you from getting out of the emotional chains that grief has put you in is addiction. Addiction will always grant you satisfaction in the short term, but you may need to watch out for its long-term implications. After experiencing a significant loss, you may pick up some addictions such as drugs, over-eating, nicotine, excessive television, caffeine, binge drinking, and so on. Although all these can make you forget your sorrow, it will only be for a while; when the pain returns, it may be worse than before. So, when you engage in addictive activities, you are not only putting yourself at risk but also slowing down your healing process.

Addiction is a severe problem that can have a devastating impact on an individual's life. It can lead to physical and mental health problems, financial and strained relationships. Fortunately, some steps can be taken to avoid becoming addicted to substances or activities.

The first step in avoiding addiction is to recognize the risk factors. People with a family history of addiction, mental health issues, or who have experienced trauma are more likely to become addicted. It is essential to be aware of these risk factors and to take steps to reduce them. This may include seeking professional help for mental health issues, avoiding triggers, and developing healthy coping skills. The second step is to practice self-care. This includes getting enough sleep, eating a healthy diet, exercising regularly, and engaging in activities that bring joy and relaxation. Taking care of oneself can help reduce stress and improve overall well-being, reducing the risk of addiction. The third step is to avoid situations that could lead to addiction. This includes avoiding places where drugs or alcohol are used, staying away from people who use drugs or alcohol, and bypassing activities that could lead to addiction. It is also essential to be aware of the signs of addiction and to seek help if needed. Finally, it is important to have a strong support system. Having a network of family and friends who can provide emotional support and guidance can be invaluable in avoiding addiction. It is also important to plan when cravings or urges arise. This could include calling a friend, walking, or engaging in a hobby. By recognizing the risk factors, practicing self-care, avoiding situations that could lead to addiction, and having a solid support system, it is possible to avoid becoming addicted to substances or activities.

To find empowerment, you need to avoid all sorts of addictions and get involved in healthy activities that can enhance your healing in the long run.

Releasing Your Emotions

Since you have made up your mind to work on your feelings by controlling them and not allowing them to control you, allowing yourself to release them into the open is one of the ways to start. Undoubtedly, the pain from grief can be difficult, but resisting it can be way more complex; therefore, you need to learn how to avoid bottling up but living with what has happened. You can do this by allowing yourself to get angry, cry, and push out negative emotions in a non-destructive but productive way to gain the strength to move along.

You should not undermine the benefits of shedding after loss, which you can do on the shoulders of those you love and trust. With this, you can clear the emotions trapped inside you. But sometimes, it may not be sorrow you feel but anger toward life. In this situation, releasing the anger via physical exercise or directing it toward a punching bag will be good. It would give you a sense of accomplishment. Soon, you will feel exhausted from the stress, so you can have time to contemplate or cry when resting.

Tips to releasing emotions are: Writing down thoughts and feelings in a journal. Writing can be a great way to get thoughts out of your head and onto paper. Breathing can help release emotions. A break from your daily routine can also give you much-needed time to relax and process emotions. Walking, listening to music, or reading a book can be great ways to take a break and release emotions. Releasing emotions is an integral part of self-care and mental health.

It would help if you always remembered to allow yourself to experience the emotions that have taken over you. As I have emphasized earlier, you should not hold back, resist, or deny them. But instead, allow them the opportunity to show you how exactly you are feeling; this is a way to your healing and empowerment.

Making a Strong Connection with Others

Even though grief is a process you feel alone inside of you, there is an option of not spending time alone. You should note this essential point because staying lonely while grieving can cause depression. So, I advise you to leave your space and connect with those you love. You can talk to them about your feelings, your emotional encounters, and how much you are missing in a healthy and supportive environment. You can also discuss the memorable times, the awkward times, the hilarious times, and the great times you had with the person you lost. The more you talk about these, the more your heavy heart will become free, paving the way for healing and moving toward becoming a better person.

In addition, sharing your thoughts and feelings with those you love can give you the strength to work through your challenges, difficult emotions, and potential struggles. A strong connection with others is to be respectful. This means treating others with kindness and respect, even if you disagree with them. It also means being willing to compromise and work together to find solutions to problems. Not only for you but also for those you share them with. Although you can manage your emotional crises in several ways, connecting with others to deal with them can make the work much more manageable; therefore, I advise you to take advantage of bonding with your loved ones.

But if you discover that you are not getting the proper strength to control your emotion, you can visit a grief counselor with whom you can also share your feelings and thoughts. Their professional duty is to offer the needed support and guide you in empowering yourself through your grief. Yes, you can get empowered through the counseling process. At the beginning stage of the process, you will be offered a distinct opportunity to explore your situation and feelings; active listening skills and the ventilation of feelings characterize the counseling process. For functional listening skills, your long-forgotten or misunderstood feelings will be brought to the surface. But for the ventilation of emotions, you will be energized, leading to spontaneous insight into unique methods of dealing with challenges that appear insurmountable.

Taking Your Health Seriously

It is a common statement that a strong body will host a strong mind. However, finding empowerment may be difficult if you allow your health to fail you while grieving. Therefore, you need to take proper care of your health while passing through emotional difficulties. A lot is happening within you – this struggle will affect your well-being.

Taking health seriously is one of the most important things for yourself. Health is the most valuable asset, and it is essential to take care of it. Taking health seriously means making healthy lifestyle choices, such as eating a balanced diet, exercising regularly, getting enough sleep, and managing stress. Awareness of potential health risks and taking steps to reduce them by eating a balanced diet is essential for good health. Eating various foods from all the food groups will give the body the nutrients it needs to function properly. Eating a balanced diet also helps maintain a healthy weight, reducing the risk of developing certain diseases. Exercising regularly is also crucial for good health. Regular physical activity helps to strengthen muscles and bones, improve cardiovascular health, and reduce stress. It can also help to improve mood and reduce the risk of developing certain diseases. Getting enough sleep is also vital for good health. Sleep helps to restore and repair the body and mind, and it can help to improve concentration. Getting enough sleep each night is essential, as not getting enough can lead to fatigue and other health problems. Managing stress is also essential for good health. Stress can harm physical and mental health, so it is crucial to find ways to manage it. This could include taking time out for yourself, engaging in relaxation activities, or talking to a friend or family member. Finally, it is important to be aware of any potential health risks and take steps to reduce them. This could include getting regular check-ups, vaccinating, and avoiding risky behaviors such as smoking or drinking too much alcohol. These steps can help reduce the risk of developing certain diseases and improve overall health.

With all these, you can give your body a suitable internal environment that supports healing to have a hassle-free journey as you shift your life for the better.

Spending Time Traveling

Sometimes, staying within an environment that triggers grief can be unhelpful. Your healing process may become more difficult as you remain, seeing things that bring more memories to the surface. So, I will advise you to take a break by traveling somewhere far away or close.

Spending time traveling is one of the most rewarding experiences a person can have. It allows you to explore new places, meet new people, and experience different cultures. Also, it is a great way to relax and unwind from the stresses of everyday life. Traveling can be a great way to learn about the world and better understand different cultures. You can visit historical sites, learn about other religions, and experience different cuisines. With traveling, you have chances to learn about the history of a place by talking to locals or meeting people from all over the world, learning about their lives, making new friends with people who share similar interests, and building relationships are a great escape. Take time to reflect on your life, gain a new perspective, and be more independent and self-reliant. It is an opportunity to gather helpful strength for the emotional healing process.

Exploring Your Creative Mind

Expressing your creativity can help you deal with your

feelings uniquely; it is an effective way to gain deeper

perspectives and insights into your existence, circumstances, and emotions. In addition, with your creative mind, you can unlock new possibilities and experiences that will enhance your emotional healing process.

There are diverse ways you can express how creative you are. If you are good with an instrument, you can do this by playing – even if you do not know how to play, you can learn. Then, you can create time to write your songs about your feelings or the loss you have experienced.

You can also write stories, poems, epistles, tributes, or even put your thoughts together in a journal. Also, if you are an artist, you can draw something that speaks of your loss or how you feel. What you do does not matter – you need to pick up something skillful enough to show how creative you are with your life crisis and emotions.

It can help tap into your innermost thoughts and feelings and express them in ways you may not have thought possible. There is a possibility to develop new skills and discover new ways of looking at the world. Creativity is a process of discovery and exploration that involves taking risks, a method of trial and error, and it can be both exciting and intimidating. Remember that creativity is not a one-time event but rather an ongoing journey. There are steps in exploring the creative mind, such as identifying creative interests. What do you enjoy doing? What do you find interesting? What do you find inspiring? Once you have identified interests, begin to explore them further.

The truth about this is that you may find yourself engaging in something you never expect; put in your best and get passionate about it. Through this, you will be amazed at how much control you will have over your emotional crisis and the strength you have called to move forward with your life.

Engaging Yourself in a Physical Way

One of the more straightforward coping mechanisms for grief is engaging in exciting and fun activities. These activities include Toastmasters, book clubs, comedy clubs, yoga, sporting events, stretching, or using exercise equipment. No matter what type of physical activity you choose, it's important to ensure you're doing it safely. Make sure you're wearing the right clothing and shoes and that you're following any safety guidelines that may be in place. If you're new to physical activity, it's also important to start slowly and gradually increasing the intensity of your workouts. It's also important to make sure you're getting enough rest and recovery time. Make sure you're getting enough sleep and taking breaks when needed. You should also ensure you're eating a balanced diet and drinking plenty of water.

You can even go all the way with learning a new skill; all the mentioned activities are just some of the numerous things you can get involved with. So, put yourself out there and do something – with this, your mind will be tentatively off your loss. In addition, you will have access to new opportunities, new perspectives, and new connections through any activities, which will help boost the speed of your emotional healing process and your emotional strength to take charge of the whole situation. With the right approach, physical activity can be a great way to stay healthy and improve your overall well-being.

Conclusion and Takeaway

The bottom line is that no matter what you may be going through, there is always a way out. All you need is to be resilient, hopeful, open to change, and strong. For grief, you must know that the way others experience grief will differ from how you will; there is no way you can account for the unique relationships and circumstances that come with grief. Besides, cultural and individual differences significantly affect how you see and deal with your loss. In addition, you already know there is no timetable or timeline for grief; when you experience loss, coming to terms with the misfortune may take a few weeks, months, or even years. Yes, I talked about some stages of grief, including denial, anger, bargaining, depression, and acceptance; but you need to know that there are no actual stages because you swing forward and backward to any of these. Nonetheless, there are three periods you will have to go through when traveling on the path of grief.

Every griever must experience the mourning period. Most time, the death of loved ones is unexpected. But even if it is expected, you will still be engulfed with disbelief and shock. There will be a transition from your usual self to a new grieving individual who is now feeling helplessness and numbness. Grief can make you feel numb and distant; as explained by psychologists, this feeling is a coping mechanism as a reaction to feeling completely overwhelmed. Some people may react with shock for sudden bursts of emotion, while others can move into isolation and introversion. Irrespective of how you may choose to respond, your emotional healing process starts once you accept that the loss has happened.

Negative emotions come with intensity; it has always been challenging for those that attempt to face them. At this phase, the feeling of heaviness from losing a loved one can appear as an unbearable burden for your heart, body, and mind. Even though it is inevitable that we will not experience grief the same way, it is understandable and expected if you feel angry, guilty, scared, and lonely. Hiding behind the reality of your loss can be a complex reaction;

it can easily be identified when you demonstrate obvious actions, including weeping, crying, sobbing, and sighing. All these are considered necessary and expected to release stress and sadness physically, but I will advise you not to bottle up your negative emotions. Repressing them usually comes with implications, which may include abuse of alcohol or drugs, appetite, and sleeping issues, difficulty concentrating, suicidal thoughts, and poor memory. If you have problems with sleeping, it can lead to rumination and insomnia, which makes the cycle of the feeling of guilt, sadness, and resentment happen repeatedly.

Medical doctors and psychologists show that several physical symptoms of biochemical and physiological reactions of grieving include absent-mindedness, tightness in the throat, a suffocating feeling, weakness in the muscles, tension, and pain. All these are meant to be dealt with, but if not, they can have terrible health implications and even surgery and hospitalization.

Finally, I advise you that amidst the waters, you should become empowered and develop the courage to find new meaning in life. Yes, the pain from losing someone you love will last for a lifetime, but you could learn how you can accept and take good advantage of your loss by pursuing achievable goals. Also, it would help if you learned how to make positive meaning out of your loss; with all these, you can quickly strengthen your connection with people around you, build on your wellness, and find your purpose in life again. Rather than invalidating the feelings of your grief, you should reconstruct and work through the narratives of your life and move along to achieve your life goals.

So, what should you take away from this book?

To understand grief and to move along, the key thing is to realize that everyone will not experience grief the same way; it is a personal experience that may give you the feeling of something different every time. Also, since there is no specific time to get over grief, you may need to deal with it for several weeks, months, or even years. But there are points you need to remember when battling an emotional crisis.

There is Light at the End of the Tunnel

Doing your best to come to terms with losing someone you love can be a journey through the darkest roads you must take in life. During grief, it is normal for you to become overwhelmed by thoughts of disbelief and hopelessness, which can make your actions toward facing reality hard. You can apply different methods to handle grief, but an unhealthy approach can cause isolation, rumination, and perhaps depression. So, you should know what you are doing when dealing with grief; with the proper steps in the emotional healing process, you can be guaranteed that there is a light at the end of the tunnel.

When grieving, you must ensure that you treat yourself with care – acknowledge that your past experiences were arduous; do all you can to avoid invalidating these experiences and your feelings. With these, you can eventually be assured of recovery soon after.

This expression is often used to refer to hope and optimism in difficult times. It is a reminder that no matter how dark and difficult the situation may seem, there is always a way out and a brighter future ahead.

This phrase is especially meaningful during times of crisis when it can be challenging to see a way forward. It is a reminder that even in the darkest times, there is hope and a chance for a better tomorrow.

Moreover, death is inevitable. When it occurs, you need to accept it and move on. Yes, you have experienced the loss of someone you love, but you have gained quite several things, such as a new perspective in life and compassion for yourself, through the event. I will say that the only thing your experience should leave you with is a sense of living a life with a purpose that your lost loved ones can be proud of.

There are unconventional methods for happiness and self-fulfillment.

It is easy to find happiness when nothing is going wrong in your life, but when a terrible life event strikes, finding happiness can be difficult. To become happy after going through some challenges, you do not need to investigate another person's life but within yourself. It is commonly said that happiness is not about you; it is its purpose through you. So, if the secret is to be happy, you need to make the purpose happen, leading to self-fulfillment.

There are many unconventional methods for happiness and self-fulfillment that can help people find joy and contentment in their lives. These methods can range from simple activities such as journaling or meditation to more complex activities such as yoga or mindfulness. Journaling is a great way to express thoughts and feelings in a safe and private space. Writing down thoughts and feelings can clarify what is causing stress or unhappiness, and it may help to identify patterns in thinking and behavior contributing to unhappiness. Meditation is another excellent way to find happiness and self-fulfillment, which reduces stress and anxiety and improves focus, concentration, and inner peace. Yoga helps to improve physical and mental health, reduce stress, and increase flexibility, contentment, and strength. Mindfulness is another great way to find happiness and self-fulfillment; it improves focus and concentration and increases self-awareness. Everyone is different, and what works for one person may not work for another. Therefore, it is essential to experiment and find what works best for you.

But there is unconventional advice I will want you to take with you —it is okay not to feel happy. This may sound odd, but it is not; the self-help culture may have tricked you into believing that happiness is always around the corner. You need to understand that, as a human being, you evolve not to be happy but to survive. So, if, due to grief, you have lost your joy, you need to understand that it is normal since you are human.

Realize that it has to run its course, and you will soon get there – accept your fate, and you will feel much better and move along.

References

1. Calhoun, L., et al. (2010). *semanticscholar.org*. Retrieved from https://www.semanticscholar.org/0b00/f1de00e4deb725dcc662cb7b67c29cbd9444.pdf&sa=U&ved=2ahUKEwjQ0ciymtf7AhVBg_0HHSM_DCgQFnoECAkQAg&usg=AOvVaw15eWIfXf6dcNTnFjw63IdP

2. BetterHelp Editorial Team. (2022, December). *betterhelp.com*. Retrieved from https://www.betterhelp.com/advice/grief/the-7-stages-of-grief-and-how-they-affect-you/

3. Davis, E. & Mohammed, S. (2017, July). *glamourmagazine.co.uk*. Retrieved from https://www.

glamourmagazine.co.uk/gallery/celebri
ties-talking-about-grief

4. Familius. (2020). *familius.com.* Retrieved from https://www. familius.com/8-famous-people-who-overcame-obstacles/

5. Scribner, H. (2014, August). *aberdeennews.com.* Retrieved from https://www. aberdeennews.com/story/entertainme nt/2014/08/04/9-famous-people-who-overcame-childhood-adversity/44970799/

6. Horsely, G. (2021, July). *forbes.com.* Retrieved from https://www.forbes.com/sites/forbesn onprofitcouncil/2021/07/28/why-grief-motivates-you-to-become-better/?sh=439dbe2b1fdd

7. Kessler, D. (2010, September). *grief.com*. Retrieved from https://www. grief.com/the-five-stages-of-grief/

8. Postel, E. & Postle, L. (2002). *griefandsympathy.com*. Retrieved from https://www. griefandsympathy.com./stories-of-grief.html

9. Beyond the Dash. (2018, December). *beyondthedash.com*. Retrieved from https://beyondthedash.com/blog/grief /signs-of-acceptance/7292

10. Vasquez, A. (2022, May). *joincake.com*. Retrieved from https://www.joincake.com/blog/motiv ation-after-a-loss/

11. KW Springer., M Carnes." Long-term physical and mental health consequences of childhood physical

abuse: Results from a large population-based sample of men and women." https://www.sciencedirect.com/science/article/pii/S0145213407000865

12. JP Forsyth." ACT on life not on anger: The new Acceptance and Commitment Therapy guide to problem anger." https://books.google.com/books?hl=en&lr=&id=X_iOvFg3I5MC&oi=fnd&pg=PR5&dq=3.+Strategies+to+Overcome+Resentment:+Practical+Ways+to+Let+Go+and+Move+On&ots=v9zNPgyVCZ&sig=S2m2BTP6F1cSjyQce91aCcRQPZM

13. GV Bodenhausen." Negative affect and social judgment: The differential impact of anger and sadness." https://onlinelibrary.wiley.com/doi/abs/10.1002/ejsp.2420240104.